The Constitution
and
Socio-Economic Change

Da Capo Press Reprints in

AMERICAN CONSTITUTIONAL AND LEGAL HISTORY

GENERAL EDITOR: LEONARD W. LEVY

Claremont Graduate School

The Constitution
and
Socio-Economic Change

Five Lectures Delivered at the University of Michigan
March 24, 25, 26, 27, and 28, 1947

By Henry Rottschaefer

Foreword by E. Blythe Stason

DA CAPO PRESS • NEW YORK • 1972

Library of Congress Cataloging in Publication Data

Rottschaefer, Henry, 1888-
The Constitution and socio-economic change.
(Da Capo Press reprints in American constitutional
and legal history)
Originally published as the 1st series of the
Thomas M. Cooley lectures.
1. Federal government — U.S. — Addresses, essays,
lectures. 2. Civil rights — U.S. — Addresses, essays,
lectures. I. Title. II. Series: Michigan.
University. Law School. The Thomas M. Cooley
lectures, 1st ser.
KF4600.A75R67   1972   342'.73'04   77-173667
ISBN 0-306-70410-2

This Da Capo Press edition of *The Constitution and Socio-Economic Change* is an unabridged republication of the first edition published in Ann Arbor, Michigan, in 1948. It is reprinted by special arrangement with the University of Michigan Law School.

Published by Da Capo Press, Inc.
A Subsidiary of Plenum Publishing Corporation
227 West 17th Street, New York, New York 10011

The Thomas M. Cooley Lectures

First Series

The Constitution and Socio-Economic Change

by

HENRY ROTTSCHAEFER

The Thomas M. Cooley Lectureship was established for the purpose of stimulating legal research and presenting its results in the form of public lectures. Thomas M. Cooley, for whom the lectureship was named, was a member of the first faculty of the University of Michigan Law School, when it was organized in 1859, and subsequently became its Dean. At the time of his death in 1898 he was one of the most distinguished legal scholars of this country. These lectures are made possible through the endowment for legal research at the University of Michigan, established by the will of the late William W. Cook, a member of the New York bar and an alumnus of the University of Michigan.

THE CONSTITUTION

AND

SOCIO-ECONOMIC CHANGE

Five lectures delivered at the University of Michigan
March 24, 25, 26, 27, and 28, 1947

by

HENRY ROTTSCHAEFER

With a Foreword by E. BLYTHE STASON
Dean, University of Michigan Law School

University of Michigan Law School
Ann Arbor   1948

To

HENRY M. BATES

In token of appreciation and regard

Contents

Foreword

By E. Blythe Stason

Every well developed system of government must embrace among its mechanisms two types of forces, first, forces to maintain the measure of stability of institutions requisite to satisfy the natural desire of citizens for continuity in their affairs; and, second, opposing forces effective to bring about necessary changes to serve changing conditions. The American Constitution, notwithstanding its precise written form, is implemented with both types of forces. Its principles are stable but they are not immutable.

James Bryce, that commentator extraordinary on our governmental institutions, observed in his treatise, *the American Commonwealth*, that the American Constitution has worn so well because, among other reasons, it has "submitted to a process of constant, though sometimes scarcely perceptible, change which has adapted it to the conditions of a new age."[1] Definitely an admirer of the American constitutional scheme, Lord Bryce found cause for sincere commendation in the rare combination of stability flowing from the written document and flexibility resulting from gradually shifting interpretation of its provisions. He recognized that flexibility is essential. Says he, in one of the earlier chapters of *the American Commonwealth*,

[1]Volume I, p. 389.

"The solemn determination of a people enacting a fundamental law by which they and their descendants shall be governed cannot prevent that law, however great the reverence they continue to profess for it, from being worn away in one part, enlarged in another, modified in a third, by the ceaseless action of influences playing upon the individuals who compose the people. Thus the American Constitution has necessarily changed as the nation has changed, has changed in the spirit with which men regard it, and therefore in its own spirit."[2]

The Viscount was a close friend of Thomas McIntyre Cooley, who, at the time *the American Commonwealth* was published in 1888, was serving as Chairman of the newly established Interstate Commerce Commission. Judge Cooley had for twenty-one years been Justice of the Supreme Court of Michigan. He was without doubt one of the most distinguished jurists in the United States and was probably the nation's most eminent constitutional lawyer. Again and again in *the American Commonwealth* Lord Bryce quoted Cooley and his writings, relying heavily upon his well-known mastery of American constitutional jurisprudence. Regarding the flexibility of the national Constitution to meet changing conditions, he quotes Judge Cooley as having observed in conversation, "We may think that we have the Constitution all before us; but for practical purposes the Constitution is that which the governmnent, in its several departments, and the people in the performance of their duties as citizens, recognize and respect as such; and nothing else is . . . "[3] In short, in 1888 each of these great

[2] *id.*
[3] *id.*

scholars clearly recognized that the American Constitution must and does possess a realistic flexibility which, kept within proper bounds, is a definite source of strength.

And yet neither Lord Bryce nor Judge Cooley, each wise as well as learned, would have overemphasized flexibility or undervalued stability. Cooley, born in 1824, admitted to the bar in 1846, selected in 1859 to be one of three members of the first faculty of the University of Michigan Law School (a post which he held until 1883), elected in 1864 to the Supreme Court of Michigan, had, in 1868, published his great treatise rather ponderously entitled *A Treatise on the Constitutional Limitations which Rest upon the Legislative Power of the States of the American Union*. It has been authoritatively written that the appearance of this volume may be accorded significance, so far as American constitutional history is concerned, not far short of another great event of 1868—the ratification of the Fourteenth Amendment to the American Constitution. Though this may be an overstatement, there is not the slightest question but that from the time of the publication of his *Constitutional Limitations* until his death in 1898, Judge Cooley was Americ'a leading authority on constitutional law. The memoirs published after his death in the 119th volume of the Michigan Supreme Court Reports reveal and record his fame.

Judge Cooley thoroughly believed in the virtues of constitutional stability. A paragraph taken from his text states his position with his usual clarity and vigor. It reads:

"A constitution is not to be made to mean one thing

at one time, and another at some subsequent time when
the circumstances may have so changed as perhaps to
make a different rule in the case seem desirable. A principal share of the benefit expected from written con-
stitutions would be lost if the rules they established
were so flexible as to bend to circumstances or be modified by public opinion. It is with special reference to the
varying moods of public opinion, and with a view to
putting the fundamentals of government beyond their
control, that these instruments are framed; . . . a court
or legislature which should allow a change in public
sentiment to influence it in giving to a written constitution a construction not warranted by the intention of its
founders, would be justly chargeable with reckless dis-
regard of official oath and public duty; and if its course
could become a precedent, these instruments would be
of little avail. The violence of public passion is quite as
likely to be in the direction of oppression as in any
other; and the necessity for bills of rights in our fundamental laws lies mainly in the danger that the legislature will be influenced, by temporary excitements and
passions among the people, to adopt oppressive enact-
ments. What a court is to do, therefore, is *to declare the
law as written*, leaving it to the people themselves to
make such changes as new circumstances may require.
The meaning of the constitution is fixed when it is
adopted, and it is not different at any subsequent time
when a court has occasion to pass upon it." [4]

Here, then, in the words of two of the most competent
scholars and observers, Lord Bryce and Judge Cooley,
is presented the age-old dilemma of government—con-

[4] p. 124.

tinuity versus change—how to reconcile the natural
desire for stability with the need of flexibility,—the
Scylla and Charybdis of constitutional jurisprudence.
Professor Rottschaefer's lectures are the first in the
series to be known as the Thomas M. Cooley Lectureship, established by the Law School of the University
of Michigan with the aid of the William W. Cook Endowment Fund. It is indeed fitting that these first lectures should deal with "The Constitution and Socio-
Economic Change." No subject could be more timely,
more significant, or more directly in the pathway of
Judge Cooley's great contributions to the American
scene.

Preface

Chief Justice Marshall as early as 1819 described the Constitution of the United States as one "intended to endure for ages to come, and, consequently, to be adapted to the various *crises* of human affairs."[1] The subsequent history of the Constitution has not always confirmed the ideal of its flexibility implicit in the Chief Justice's statement. There have been periods during which the courts, the principal agency in the adaptative process, have resisted change by invalidating legislation implementing popular demand for reforms based on political and socio-economic philosophies in conflict with those implicit in prior judicial constructions of the Constitution. The constitutional revision that has occurred since 1933 furnishes a dramatic illustration of such a contest between the courts and the popular demand for social reform. The discussion that follows has aimed not only to describe and analyze the process by which constitutional adaptation occurred during the crisis induced by the most severe economic depression of modern times, but also to develop the implications of the constitutional theories and doctrines that constitute the constitutional law of today. The scope of this study does not include the impact upon our governmental system of the decisions resulting from the war, and that may be rendered in

[1] McCulloch v. Maryland, 4 Wheat. 316, 4 L. Ed. 579 (1819).

passing on the validity of measures adopted during the reconstruction period whose end is not yet in sight. It is quite likely that the changes actually discussed will prove to define only the minimum scope of constitutional revision that will occur before the process of adaptation achieves a recognizable degree of stable equilibrium.

Henry Rottschaefer

University of Minnesota
Minneapolis, Minnesota
January, 1948.

The Constitution and Socio-Economic Change

Introduction

THE economic crisis and depression that afflicted the nation in varying degrees of intensity from 1929 until the outbreak of World War II coincided with an extremely unstable political and economic situation throughout the world. It was a period when many nations were imposing restrictions upon the freedom of international trade in their desire to achieve self-sufficiency. The United States was a creditor nation during a great part of this period, but, despite that, persisted in following tariff policies adapted to a nation that was a debtor on the balance of international payments. Our economy revealed a high state of imbalance. The price deflation proceeded at an uneven rate with respect to the various groups of commodities. The position of debtors, especially those bound by long-term commitments, became so serious as to create dangers to the community. The demand for government intervention to mitigate the consequences of the normal methods of readjustment became too insistent to be ignored. The result was a flood of legislation at both the state and federal levels, much of which proceeded on what were deemed by many quite unorthodox methods. It trenched on vested rights in a manner not wholly new but with an intensity that was somewhat novel. Much of it reflected political, economic, and social philosophies that clashed violently with those that had prevailed during the period of the nation's industrial expansion that began soon after the Civil War. Laissez faire had dominated that era, and that government was deemed best which governed least. The implications of these theories had influenced the judicial construction of those provisions of the federal Constitution that limited the powers of both the state and federal governments. This was especially true of the due process clause of the Fourteenth Amendment. While inroads had been made upon them, they were still fairly vigorous factors in shaping judicial decisions up to the time of the great depression of the thirties.

The depression produced a serious collapse of private individual initiative. It could not maintain its position in the face of idle plant, mass unemployment, deflation, and bank holidays. All these involved hardships and losses greater than those who endured them were willing to bear if there was any way out. Government intervention was sought and given. The financial burden of relieving distress was beyond the fiscal capacities of the individual states, and the federal government assumed an increasing part of the cost. At the same time there occurred important shifts in opinion as to the causes of the debacle. The view that the causes were nationwide induced a demand for federal intervention. Remedies were freely suggested, all based on purported analyses of the causes responsible for the existing situation. The theories that gained widest currency and acceptance by responsible officials were that the nation's productive capacity had outstripped its power successfully to distribute the goods and services produced; that there was a lack of effective purchasing power that could be cured only by governmental redistribution of income; and that the chaos, inherent in what was described as the private enterprise system, was responsible for the violent ups and downs of the business cycle, and could be avoided only by moving in the direction of a planned economy. The soundness of such views is quite immaterial.[1] Their widespread acceptance in a democratic society was bound to produce an increase in governmental activities. I have summarized the effects of these movements and speculations elsewhere in the following language:

"The net effect has been a shift in political, economic and social philosophies from individualism towards socialism, from acceptance of an economic system operating in response to the profit motive to belief in one in which government planning and direction is to play an increased role, from a social philosophy which admitted the duty of government to intervene in the distribution of income to a limited extent to one urging government to interpose for that purpose on an ever-increasing scale, and from a politi-

1. The orthodox explanation of the debacle of 1929, and the depression whose beginnings it marked, would have stressed the national and international maladjustments following World War I; the uneven effects of the 1920–1921 deflation which was especially severe on agricultural products and raw materials generally; the presence in the post-World War I period of monopolistic elements in both the national and world economy, some of them the result of private agreement and others originating in governmental actions; the waste of savings in what proved to be misdirected investments and in speculation; the inflationary methods employed to finance World War I, and much of the speculation that followed in its wake; attempts by nations to achieve economic autarchy with the consequent barriers to restoring international trade; and a generally unstable political situation throughout large areas of the world. That approach was rather cavalierly brushed aside as outmoded in favor of one that relied heavily upon the economic and monetary theories of the English economist John Maynard Keynes as these were adopted by American economists to support the legislative program of the New Deal.

cal and constitutional theory of rather restricted federal
activity to one in which the federal government was assigned the major role in realizing the social objectives explicit or implicit in the new approaches to our social and
economic problems."²

The legislative programs enacted to combat the depression and to alleviate its consequences were bound
to trench on many vested interests, and to raise important issues concerning the division of governmental
powers between the Nation and the States. It was inevitable that the Supreme Court would have to dispose
of them. That the social forces back of the insistent
demand that government do something would affect
the course of its decisions was a belief justified by history. Predictions as to how far it would adapt its construction of the Constitution to them would have been
hazardous. The changes in opinion that have been described did not introduce wholly novel elements into
our political, economic, and social philosophies. The
most extreme advocate of laissez faire never claimed
that government should adopt a complete hands-off
policy with respect to the economic system. On the
contrary, he was a firm believer in its duty to preserve
the peace, protect property, enforce contracts, and generally maintain those legal institutions that were the
legal foundations of a private enterprise economy. Government redistribution of income was as old as the poor
laws, and had already gone quite far when the depression arrived. The changes in our philosophical presup-
positions represented shifts in emphasis rather than the

2. Rottschaefer, The Constitution and a "Planned Economy," 38 Mich.
Law Rev. 1133, 1134 (1940).

adoption of a completely new set of assumptions. They did not reflect a general demand for a new society on the basis of wholly new political, social, and economic philosophies. In fact, the professed aim of the leaders in the movement to use the law as an instrument for changing the structure of society by reference to a new scale of values was to preserve the system of individual private enterprise by making it work more efficiently and more in the social interest. The objective was not revolution but adaptation to values reflecting a change of emphasis. The Supreme Court, confronted with the task of deciding whether the Constitution permitted the legal adjustments being made by legislation, could either ignore the principles theretofore developed or, accepting them, reinterpret them in applying them to new situations. It was probable that it would choose the latter course. It has, in form at least, generally done so. Even when overruling established precedents, it has at times treated them as departures from the true construction of the Constitution. To overrule them was, therefore, a reinstatement of the true doctrine.[3]

The aim of what follows will be to consider the response of the Supreme Court to the opportunity presented it when confronted with the constitutional issues raised by the depression legislation. It will be necessary also to take account of its revisions of other established

3. See, for example, the following language of Justice Stone in United States v. Darby, (1941) 312 U.S. 100, 116, 117, concerning Hammer v. Dagenhart, (1918) 247 U.S. 251, which was expressly overruled therein: "The conclusion is inescapable that *Hammer* v. *Dagenhart*, was a departure from the principles which have prevailed in the interpretation of the Commerce Clause both before and since the decision and that such vitality, as a precedent, as it then had has long since been exhausted. It should be and now is overruled."

principles where these are in line with the general trend evidenced by its decisions in the former field. In analyzing and evaluating its work, it will be necessary to trace the prior development of those principles invoked in support of its decisions. Those were the tools it employed to accomplish its transformation of the Constitution into what it now has become. The theories developed by it in the course of its reformulation of constitutional doctrines demand careful attention. They are an essential part of the practicing lawyer's equipment. He must be familiar with them and their use if his advice is to be sound within the limits set by the nature of the subject matter. The general implications of what has happened are even more important. The Constitution is both a grant of powers and a limitation upon their exercise by both the federal government and the states. Its interpretation defines the limits within which government may act, and thus determines the areas of permissible individual action and individual freedom so far as these are functions of governmental regulation.

I

Development of Federal Powers Prior to 1933

THE Constitution of the United States was ratified by the last state requisite for its adoption in 1788. Its adoption was in large measure a response to the need for a more effective union among the states than had theretofore existed. Their cooperation in waging a successful war of independence, and during the brief period thereafter under the Articles of Confederation, had revealed important defects. The provisions of the Articles furnished practically no basis for the effective regulation of what were matters of general and common interest even in the relatively simple social and economic conditions of that day. The obstacles to interstate trade resulting from the numerous and conflicting state regulations gave a strong impetus to movements to amend the Articles. It is unnecessary to trace the various steps which ultimately led to the adoption of the Constitution. The important matter for present purposes is that it provided for the establishment of a government capable of acting upon the people of the several states directly without invoking the intervention of the governments of the states,[1] and that it conferred upon that

1. This was the position of Chief Justice Marshall in McCulloch v. Maryland, (1819) 4 Wheat. 316. In Ex parte Siebold, (1886) 100 U.S. 371, 395,

government certain powers, while leaving to the several states the exercise of the residue of the sovereign powers belonging to the people of the United States. A legal basis had been furnished for welding the states and their peoples into a single nation under the newly established government. There was no assurance that this would happen, and a prediction as to the lines along which that government would develop would have been extremely hazardous. The present size, complexity, and scope of powers exercised by the federal government, represent the end product as of today of a long and tortuous process that began almost immediately after the adoption of the Constitution. The steps in that process, the factors that influenced it, and the theories and rationalizations evolved to explain it must all be analyzed to determine the implications for the future of its more recent stages.

A federal system, such as the Constitution established, raises difficult problems concerning the distribution of governmental power between the nation and the states. If the powers of the latter are residual, their scope necessarily depends upon whether a broad or narrow construction is applied to the grants of power to the nation. The plan set forth in the Constitution was of this type. The Constitution did not meet with universal acceptance. Nor did all those who had approved it, and worked for its ratification, agree as to its nature or its interpretation. The Federalists favored

---

Justice Bradley phrased it in the following language: "We hold it to be an incontrovertible principle, that the government of the United States may, by means of physical force, exercised through its official agents, execute on every foot of American soil the powers and functions that belong to it."

a construction that would promote the development of a strong national government. The Republicans advocated a narrow interpretation which would preserve a broader field of action for the states. The struggle between them appeared under various guises depending upon the character of the issue involved. In 1803 the Supreme Court decided the case of *Marbury v. Madison*[2] and announced the doctrine that the final interpretation of the Constitution lay with the judicial department as incident to its duty of deciding cases and controversies within its jurisdiction in accordance with the applicable law, including the Constitution. The Court was at that time controlled by Federalists, whose theories continued to dominate it as long as Chief Justice Marshall remained a member. That decision afforded Marshall the opportunity to give to his interpretations of the Constitution an authority that future justices would have to take into account even in their disagreements with his theories. He took full advantage of his opportunities, and received able assistance, especially from Justice Story who, though nominally a Republican, had been completely won over to Marshall's point of view. Justice Story had in *Martin v. Hunter's Lessee*,[3] decided in 1816, forcefully rejected the claim that the Constitution had been ordained and established by the states acting in their sovereign capacity in favor of the view that it was an act of the people of the United States. The Court in that case sustained its own power to review the decisions of state courts on matters of federal constitutional law. The same view as to the

2. (1803) 1 Cr. 137.
3. (1816) 1 Wheat. 304.

source of the Constitution was set forth by Marshall in *McCulloch v. Maryland.*[4] The facts of this case are so familiar as to require no statement here. Counsel for the State of Maryland had contended that in the construction of the Constitution that instrument should be considered "not as emanating from the people, but as the act of sovereign and independent States," and that the powers of the general government had been "delegated by the States, who alone are truly sovereign; and must be exercised in subordination to the States, who alone possess supreme dominion." The Chief Justice refuted this in his opinion and concluded that "The government of the Union, then, . . . is, emphatically, and truly, a government of the people. In form and in substance it emanates from them. Its powers are granted by them, and are to be exercised directly on them, and for their benefit." The view that the Constitution was not the result of an agreement among the states but the product of an act of the sovereign people of the United States establishing a national government for the attainment of national objectives thus became an important element in our constitutional theory. The ultimate development of the national government into what it has become today minimizes the importance of the dissent that met Marshall's views when he was formulating them.

It was also during Marshall's term of office that the Federalist theory of a broad construction of federal powers became an established principle of our constitutional law. The opinion of the Chief Justice in *McCulloch v. Maryland* gave it definite formulation, and the

4. (1819) 4 Wheat. 316, 402–405.

decision therein gave it its first important application. The issue before the Court was the power of the State of Maryland to tax the note issue power of the second Bank of the United States, a private corporation created by Congress. The power of Congress to incorporate a bank or any corporation whatever was denied by the State, but sustained by reasoning that has remained a classic exposition of the Federalist position. The principle that the federal government is one of delegated powers is unreservedly accepted, but its supremacy within its field of action is firmly asserted. Admitting that the establishment of a bank or creating a corporation is not found among the "enumerated powers," the Constitution is held to confer upon Congress implied powers to "employ the necessary means, for the execution of the powers conferred on the government." This is rightly supported by reliance upon its power of making "all laws which shall be necessary and proper, for carrying into execution the foregoing powers, and all other powers vested by this constitution, in the government of the United States, or in any department thereof." That the same result would have been reached had the Constitution contained no such provision is clear from much of the reasoning that preceded the Court's express reliance upon it. The attempt to give that provision a restrictive operation was rejected in favor of one that has made it an important factor in the expansion of federal powers. An important consideration urged in support of this view was that its subject "is the execution of those great powers on which the welfare of a nation essentially depends"; that those who gave those powers must have intended "to insure

. . . their beneficial execution," which could not have been done by confining the "choice of means to such narrow limits as not to leave it in the power of Congress to adopt any which might be appropriate, and which were conducive to the end"; and that any other construction would be out of place in a "constitution intended to endure for ages to come, and, consequently, to be adapted to the various *crises* of human affairs." The idea recurs throughout the opinion that it is for Congress to select the means for implementing the delegated powers so as to attain the objectives of the Constitution. The broad sweep of the argument is aptly summarized in the following quotation from the opinion:

> "We admit, as all must admit, that the powers of the government are limited, and that its limits are not to be transcended. But we think the sound construction of the constitution must allow to the national legislature that discretion, with respect to the means by which the powers it confers are to be carried into execution, which will enable that body to perform the high duties assigned to it, in the manner most beneficial to the people. Let the end be legitimate, let it be within the scope of the constitution, and all means which are appropriate, which are plainly adapted to that end, which are not prohibited, but consist with the letter and spirit of the constitution, are constitutional."[5]

It was also explicitly stated that the Court had no power to trespass on the domain of the legislature by inquiring into the degree of necessity of the means selected by Congress. This was undoubtedly in answer to the contention of counsel for the State of Maryland that, however necessary a national bank might have been when

5. At p. 421 of 4 Wheat.

there were but few banks in the nation, it could no longer be considered such in view of the adequate banking facilities furnished by state banking systems. The basis of that part of the opinion devoted to the power of Congress to incorporate the Bank represented not only a sweeping triumph for the nationalist point of view but also for the power of Congress to select the instruments for achieving national objectives with a minimum of judicial supervision. No firmer foundation could have been laid for an expansion of federal powers should changing circumstances make such a development appear desirable. The spiritual ancestor of those who have sanctioned their recent extension was Chief Justice Marshall.

It has taken more than a century to develop the implications of this position to a point involving an almost revolutionary shift in governmental power within the nation. The process has not been a continuous evolution in this direction. At the time when *McCulloch v. Maryland* was decided, and for a long period thereafter, the social and economic activities of the people were regulated predominantly by the states. The constitutional issues coming before the Supreme Court during this period were concerned principally with defining the powers of the states as affected by the grant of power to the federal government and the express limitations on the states, such as those found in Article I, Section 10, of the Constitution. The limits based on the commerce clause are the most important for our purposes. The first case to be decided by the Supreme Court in this field was *Gibbons v. Ogden*.[6] The State of

6. (1824) 9 Wheat. 1.

New York had conferred upon Ogden's assignors a monopoly to operate steamboats between New York City and various New Jersey points which he sought to protect against invasion by Gibbons who was operating between New York City and some of the same New Jersey points under a federal license to engage in the coasting trade. The narrow point decided was that the state grant of the monopoly was invalid for conflict with the federal statute under which Gibbons obtained his license. But its real importance is that it initiated a long controversy in the Supreme Court as to the nature of the commerce power and the extent to which it affected the powers of the states. There were at that time sharp differences of opinion on whether it was an exclusive or a concurrent power. Both views were vigorously presented by counsel for the parties to the controversy. Chief Justice Marshall, who wrote the principal opinion in the case, definitely inclined to the former view but felt it unnecessary to determine the matter, stating that there was great force in the argument that had been made for it and that "the Court is not satisfied that it has been refuted." The reason why he felt it unnecessary to go further was that, in cases in which a conflict existed between a state regulation of its purely internal affairs and a valid exercise of federal power, the former must yield "whether those laws were passed in virtue of a concurrent power 'to regulate commerce with foreign nations and among the several States,' or, in virtue of a power to regulate their domestic trade and police."[7]

The supremacy of federal powers over state powers

7. At p. 210 of 9 Wheat.

here asserted was not denied even at this early date. Under decisions of a much later period the limits imposed on the states by the mere existence of the commerce clause have been developed to include state regulation irrespective of the state power being exercised. The conflict of opinion as to the nature of the commerce clause continued unabated. Chief Justice Marshall never did commit himself on the issue. He did, however, sustain a Delaware statute which authorized the construction of a dam across a navigable water of the United States despite the fact that the dam obstructed navigation.[8] The basis for the decision was that, "under all the circumstances of the case" the state Act authorizing it could not "be considered as repugnant to the power to regulate commerce in its dormant state, or as being in conflict with any law passed on the subject."[9] The substantial considerations influencing the decision were of a character that would be described today as relevant to determining whether an exercise of a state's police power did, or did not, impose an undue burden upon interstate commerce. It is significant that he did not justify the state Act as an exercise of a power to regulate interstate commerce retained by the state as he might easily have done had he then believed such concurrent power to exist. In his dissent in the *Mayor, etc. of the City of New York v. Miln*,[10] Justice Story accepted the exclusive nature of the commerce power without reservations, and asserted Chief Justice Marshall's entire concurrence in his dissent.[11] However, the

8. Wilson v. Black Bird Creek Marsh Co., (1829) 2 Pet. 412.
9. At p. 252 of 2 Pet.
10. (1837) 11 Pet. 102.
11. At p. 160 of 11 Pet.

conflict of opinion was finally resolved in *Cooley v. Board of Port Wardens, etc.*[12]

The solution arrived at in that case was a compromise. The focal point of discussion was shifted from the nature of the commerce power to the nature of the "subjects of this power." The logic of Justice Curtis' argument has no permanent value or interest. The conclusions derived from it have furnished an approach to the problem of the validity of state regulations of, or affecting, interstate commerce that is still available. The subjects of the power were divided into those which are "in their nature national, or admit only of one uniform system, or plan of regulation" and those which do not require "exclusive legislation, but may be best provided for" by the States as local circumstances may dictate. No adequate tests have yet been devised for assigning a given subject of regulation to its proper class. In time the theory gave rise to several baffling problems. The Court referred to the fact that Congressional legislation manifested an intention not only not to regulate the matters involved in the case but also to leave their regulation to the states. The reference was to an Act of 1789 leaving the regulation of pilots to state laws then in force or thereafter enacted. It is explicitly stated that the opinion is not to be extended to the "question what other subjects, under the commercial power . . . may be regulated by the States in the absence of all congressional legislation; nor to the general question how far any regulation of a subject by Congress, may be deemed to operate as an exclusion of all legislation by the States

12. (1851) 12 How. 299.

upon the same subject."[13] The Court here clearly antic-
ipated the problems of the effect of the silence of Congress, and of its partial occupation of a field of regulation, upon state power to act. Later decisions have
developed general rules for dealing with such situations,
but the difficulties inhering in their application have not
diminished. ,

The conflict in the Court as to the nature of the commerce power was but one aspect of a wider struggle
between advocates of a strong national government and
those who feared such a development as a threat to the
states. The logical implications of the exclusive power
theory would have severely limited the states' powers
in the absence of some other basis on which their regulation of transactions constituting a part of interstate
or foreign commerce might have been rested. The extent
of the restrictions would increase as the power to regulate interstate and foreign commerce expanded. During
this very period the power to regulate foreign commerce
had been held to include the sale in the original package
of goods imported from abroad. A state license tax on
the sale of imports in that form by importers and wholesalers had been held invalid for conflict with the commerce clause.[14] The opinion in that case had stated
that the Court supposed "the principles laid down in
this case, to apply equally to importations from a sister
State." While the later extension is no part of the constitutional law of today,[15] the mere suggestion must have

13. At p. 320 of 12 How.
14. Brown v. Maryland, (1827) 12 Wheat. 419.
15. The history of attempts to use the "original package doctrine" as a
limit on the power of the states to tax goods introduced into one state from
another state can be traced in the following decisions: Woodruff v. Parham,

aroused the fears of those who were battling against the centralizing tendencies of Chief Justice Marshall's theories. That their fears were not groundless appeared much later when the "original package doctrine" was used by the Court to interpose serious obstacles to the efforts of the states to enforce various sorts of prohibitory and other regulatory police measures.[16] It is only recently that it has lost at least some of its importance in this field, and there is no guaranty against its revival.[17] Moreover, its loss of status has been due largely to the development of new approaches for determining when state regulations violate the commerce clause.

With the expansion of the national economy that followed the close of the Civil War, there was a marked increase in interstate commerce. There was no corresponding expansion of its regulation by Congress. The states, in order to protect what they conceived to be their legitimate interests, enacted legislation of their own for that purpose. Some of this involved a direct regulation of interstate commerce; the subject matter of some of it was purely local transactions. State quarantine and inspection laws applied to goods being transported in interstate commerce into or through a state are an example of the former. Chief Justice Marshall had recognized in *Gibbons v. Ogden* that the states had retained the power to regulate their purely domestic trade and police, but had at the same time affirmed that their

(1869) 8 Wall. 123; Askren v. Continental Oil Co., (1920) 252 U.S. 444; Bowman v. Continental Oil Co., (1921) 256 U.S. 642; Texas Co. v. Brown, (1922) 258 U.S. 466; Sonneborn Bros. v. Cureton, (1923) 262 U.S. 506.

16. See *infra*, pp. 122–126.

17. See opinion of Justice Cardozo in Baldwin v. Seelig, (1935) 294 U.S. 511.

exercise of this power would be invalid if in conflict with legislation enacted by Congress under its commerce power. In the *License Cases* state regulation of the sale of intoxicants had been sustained as an exercise of the states' police power even as applied to original package sales of liquors imported from another state.[18] In an early case involving a state quarantine against cattle from other states, the Court formulated its approach to the constitutional issue in the following language:

> "It seems hardly necessary to argue at length, that, unless the statute can be justified as a legitimate exercise of the police power of the State, it is a usurpation of the power vested exclusively in Congress. It is a plain regulation of inter-state commerce, a regulation extending to prohibition."[19]

The Court's opinion is replete with confused contradictions. A strong affirmation of the exclusive nature of the commerce power is followed by the statement that the grant of that power to Congress "was not a surrender of that which may properly be denominated police power." It admits that a state may exercise that power by completely excluding certain persons and commodities, and avoids the appearance of contradiction by inventing the theory that this would not be regulation of interstate commerce, "in the constitutional sense of the term." A regulation is one "in the constitutional sense" if it goes "beyond what is absolutely necessary" for the state's protection. The quarantine statute was held invalid for that reason, and not because it was a regulation of interstate commerce. Subsequent deci-

18. (1847) 5 How. 504.
19. Railroad Company v. Husen, (1878) 95 U.S. 465.

sions have sustained such state acts which went no further than necessary to protect what were recognized as legitimate state interests.[20] The actual process employed was one of balancing the national interest in freedom of interstate trade against that which the state was seeking to protect by its restriction upon such commerce. As is every choice between alternative objectives, it is an evaluative process.

The principal method used by courts in this field has followed this general pattern. It is, in fact, the only one available where the state legislation can not be considered as a regulation of transactions that are a part of interstate commerce under any likely definition of that term. In such case the analysis derived from *Cooley v. Board of Port Wardens* would be wholly inapplicable. *Sioux Remedy Company v. Cope*[21] may be taken as an example. A state statute required foreign corporations to file a copy of their charter with a state official as a condition precedent to transacting any business within it, or maintaining a suit in its courts, and denied access to its courts to any corporation failing to qualify, even to enforce the collection of the price of goods sold within the state in an interstate sale. The statute as thus applied was held to violate the commerce clause. The Court expressly refrained from holding the right to demand and enforce payment for goods thus sold to be a part of interstate commerce, but stated that it, "if not

20. Missouri, Kansas & Texas R. Co. v. Haber, (1898) 169 U.S. 613; Smith v. St. L. & S.W. R. Co., (1901) 181 U.S. 248; Compagnie Trans-Atlantique v. Bd. of Health, etc., (1902) 186 U.S. 380; Asbell v. Kansas, (1908) 209 U.S. 251. See Rottschaefer, Handbook of American Constitutional Law, Secs. 153–156.

21. (1914) 235 U.S. 197. For a later case that impliedly restricts the scope of that decision, see Union Brokerage Co. v. Jensen, (1944) 322 U.S. 202.

a part of such commerce, is so directly connected with it and is so essential to its existence and continuance that the imposition of unreasonable conditions upon this right must necessarily operate as a restraint or burden upon interstate commerce." In *Davis v. Farmers' Co-op Equity Company*,[22] a state statute prescribing the method of commencing actions in its courts against foreign corporations was held invalid as imposing an undue burden upon interstate commerce where the cause of action had not arisen in the state, the transaction out of which the suit arose had not been entered into in it, the defendant interstate railroad neither owned nor operated any railroad within it, and the state was not that of plaintiff's residence. The waste of time and money involved in permitting a state to try suits under such circumstances was held to constitute an unreasonable burden upon interstate commerce. Later decisions dealing with the "imported suit" problem have balanced against the burden they placed on commerce that which would be imposed upon the plaintiff were the action not allowed, and have in some instances permitted it to be maintained.[23]

Reference to a wholly different type of regulation will show the pervasiveness of this approach. The function of interstate trade in consumers' goods is to enable producers in one state to market them in other states. The retail sale is ordinarily the final step in the process. That sale has never been considered a transaction in interstate

22. (1923) 262 U.S. 312.
23. See Missouri ex rel. St. L., B. & M. R. Co. v. Taylor, (1924) 266 U.S. 200; Hoffman v. Missouri, (1927) 274 U. S. 21; Mich Cent. R. Co. v. Mix, (1929) 278 U.S. 492; International Milling Co. v. Columbia Transp. Co., (1934) 292 U.S. 511.

commerce, not even when made in the original package in which it was introduced into the state of ultimate sale. It is a purely local transaction. The commerce clause, however, protects that sale, whether or not it be made in the original package, from state regulation whose purpose is to discriminate against interstate commerce or to establish "an economic barrier against competition with the products of another state or the labor of its residents."[24] While the technique here described is the only one developed where the state regulates transactions that are not part of interstate commerce, the quarantine cases show that it can be, and has been, used where the regulated transaction is one in such commerce as that has been judicially defined. It is now, and has been for a long time, the principal method used by courts in that field. The analysis and approach of *Cooley v. Board of Port Wardens* today plays at most a minor part in reaching decisions even in the limited field defined by its own terms.

It is apparent that the weighing of the interest which the state regulation aims to protect against those which the commerce clause was adopted to secure necessarily forces courts to make decisions on important matters of policy. This cannot be avoided as long as they are charged with the task of reconciling or choosing between competing interests. The existence, character, and extent of the effects of a regulation are undoubtedly questions of fact. And in many instances evidence thereof must be, and is, before the Court. But they furnish but one element in the judgment that must be made in deciding cases in this field. Unless it be assumed

24. Baldwin v. Seelig, (1935) 294 U.S. 511.

that the mere existence of any effects tending to reduce the flow of interstate trade suffices to render the regulation invalid, the problem becomes one of degree. Courts have never adopted this extreme position. The normal result of a regulation that increases either the cost of producing goods for the interstate market, or the cost of their transportation in interstate commerce, would be a reduction in the volume of such commerce. Yet the Supreme Court has stated more than once that a state tax having that effect does not violate the commerce clause on that account. Judicial recognition that the protection of some state interests justifies a larger interference with interstate trade than does the protection of others further complicates the matter. No court has yet devised any scale for measuring the relative values of freedom of interstate trade and the numerous local interests which a state may wish to protect at the former's expense. This is not necessarily a disadvantage. It has facilitated adapting the commerce clause to changing social and economic needs and philosophies. This is not a new phenomenon peculiar to our own times. The shift of judicial opinion on the issue of the exclusive or concurrent nature of the commerce clause was not uninfluenced by factors present in the political and economic environment of the period. No one would doubt that this process would have occurred had the power of construing the commerce clause been vested in Congress alone. History has proved that the Supreme Court has responded to the impact of the same necessity and forces. No one would question that, on the assumption just made, the interpretations of Congress inevitably would have involved value judgments. The need for them cannot be eliminated by conferring the power of final construction of the commerce clause, and, for that matter, most other provisions of the Constitution, upon the judiciary. This has been accomplished through employing such concepts as "direct burden," "undue burden," and, more recently, "substantial burden" to describe the invalidating factor. The first of these expressions has been subjected to severe criticism, especially recently,[25] but it may well be questioned whether the substitution for it of the last one has contributed very much, if anything, to either the formulation of the problem, its understanding, or its solution.

Chief Justice Marshall's statement in *Gibbons v. Ogden* that a federal regulation of interstate or foreign commerce invalidated any state regulation in conflict therewith, whether referable to a concurrent power to regulate interstate commerce or its power to regulate local trade and police, has already been mentioned. It was not long thereafter that he applied the same principle to the states' power to tax in *Brown v. Maryland*.[26] The tax was imposed upon importers and wholesalers of imported merchandise that had paid import duties under federal law. The case involved an importer selling goods in the original package in which they had been imported. The import duties were treated as the price paid for the privilege not only of importation but also of selling the import. The state tax was thus held to conflict with an exercise of Congress' power to regulate foreign commerce. The supremacy of that power over

25. See, for example, the concurring opinion of Justice Rutledge in Freeman v. Hewit, (1946) 329 U.S. 249.
26. (1827) 12 Wheat. 419.

a state's taxing power had been vigorously contested by counsel for Maryland. The Court repelled the attack with the statement that this taxing power may not "be used so as to obstruct the free course of a power given to Congress" nor "to obstruct or defeat the power to regulate commerce." The "original package doctrine" was invented to define the duration of an import's immunity from state taxation. Subsequent decisions have given it specific content for other situations, and it remains in good standing to this day.[27] Although the Court's reasoning relies heavily upon the fact that the imports had paid duties, there is no reason to believe that the decision would have been different had the goods entered the United States duty free. The opinion states that the Court supposes "the principles laid down in this case, to apply equally to importations from a sister State." It can be assumed that any protective tariff levied by a state on interstate imports would have been held invalid when *Brown v. Maryland* was decided. If that be correct, then the application of the principles of that case to interstate trade could not have been limited to articles that had paid a duty levied by the importing state. Since it would be inconceivable that the Court intended interstate commerce to be entitled to a larger immunity from state taxation than that granted foreign commerce, it follows that it did not intend to limit the

27. The latest discussion of it by the Supreme Court is in Hooven & Allison v. Evatt, (1945) 324 U.S. 652, rehearing denied, (1945) 325 U.S. 892. This case involved imports from both foreign countries and the Phillipine Islands. Four of the Justices agreed that the state tax in question was invalid as applied to both classes of imports. These four and Justice Reed constituted the majority with respect to the tax on imports from foreign countries. The same four and Justice Murphy constituted the majority with respect to the imports from the Phillipine Islands.

decision to foreign imports that had paid federal duties. The principle implicit in much of Chief Justice Marshall's reasoning is that the commerce clause itself operates as a limit on the states' power to tax. Later decisions have abundantly sustained this position. The "original package doctrine," however, after a varied career, has long since ceased being a limit on the states' power to tax interstate imports.[28]

It is doubtful that any of those who participated in deciding *Brown v. Maryland* envisaged any considerable part of the developments of its fundamental principle. As the national economy became more integrated the opportunities for invoking it increased. This process proceeded at an accelerated pace following the Civil War. The number of cases reaching the Supreme Court which involved such issues increased greatly. The increased revenue needs of the states led them to tap new sources of income. It was a practical certainty that each new tax would ultimately have its validity determined by the Supreme Court. There was present also another factor. Acceptance of the principle of the protective tariff, and the desire to hamper the competition of outsiders, seem almost instinctive. The taxing power is a convenient instrument for implementing such policies. That states, and even their local political subdivisions, have frequently used it for those ends is obvious. The correctness of an interpretation of the commerce clause invalidating such attempts is equally obvious. The Supreme Court has, accordingly, always held invalid state taxes that discriminated against interstate commerce. It has been diligent in finding such discrimina-

28. See note 15, *supra*.

tion even though the statute imposing the tax was not discriminatory on its face. But its decisions have gone far beyond that point. Taxes levied primarily, and sometimes wholly, for revenue purposes have not escaped being held to violate the implied restrictions of the commerce clause.[29] The theory of these decisions was that taxation was a form of regulation as much subject to those restrictions as were those predicated upon the police power. There is no particular objection to describing taxation of, or which affects, interstate commerce as a regulation thereof. Taxes have regulatory effects, whether or not the legislature intends them. But they are also the ultimate means for defraying the costs of government. This latter aspect cannot be ignored in deciding whether a state tax transgresses the implied limitations of the commerce clause. The Court has never explicitly denied it some recognition, but only recently has it begun to receive the emphasis to which it is entitled.[30] This change in the judicial approach to the issue of the validity of state taxes has not enabled the Court to reach easy solutions in particular cases. It indicates merely an increased appreciation of one of the significant factors of the problem. The observations made in discussing the similar problem in respect to the state's police power apply here also. The expressions used in that connection to summarize the results of the

29. There is no evidence that purposes other than revenue were any factor in state imposition of property taxes on goods moving in interstate commerce, yet those have been invariably held invalid; Carson Petroleum Co. v. Vial, (1929) 279 U. S. 95. The same statement is true with respect to franchise taxes imposed on corporations exclusively engaged in interstate or foreign commerce within the taxing state; Ozark Pipe Line Corp. v. Monier, (1925) 266 U. S. 555.

30. See discussion in Chapter III, *infra*.

evaluative process necessarily involved are used also in the decisions as to the effect of the commerce clause upon the states' power to tax.

The restrictive effects of the commerce clause, even as ameliorated by the principles of *Cooley v. Board of Port Wardens* and the recognition of the states' police powers, interfered frequently with the effective execution of important state policies. A situation finally arose that led to Congressional intervention to relieve the states of some of the then existing restraints on their powers. During the seventies and eighties of the last century several midwestern states had prohibited the manufacture and sale of intoxicating beverages. The enforcement of this policy against interstate sales,[31] and local original package sales of intoxicants brought in from other states,[32] was held to conflict with the commerce clause. Their appeals to Congress led to the enactment of the Wilson Act in 1890, which subjected intoxicants to the laws of those states upon their arrival therein. The validity of that Act was a fairly debatable matter when the issue came before the Supreme Court. In *Gibbons v. Ogden*, Chief Justice Marshall, in meeting the contention that the Pilot Act of August 7, 1789, impliedly acknowledged a concurrent power in the states to regulate interstate commerce, had stated that "Congress cannot enable a State to legislate" but might adopt the provisions of state laws on any subject. In *Cooley v. Board of Port Wardens*, Justice Curtis drew from the enactment of that Act the very conclusion

31. Bowman v. Chicago & N.W. Ry. Co., (1888) 125 U.S. 465.
32. Leisy v. Hardin, (1890) 135 U.S. 100.

that Chief Justice Marshall had denied. In his opinion, he had used the following language:

> "If the States were divested of the power to legislate on this subject [of pilotage] by the grant of the commercial power to Congress, it is plain this act could not confer upon them power thus to legislate. If the Constitution excluded the States from making any law regulating commerce, certainly Congress cannot regrant it, or in any manner reconvey to the States that power."[33]

When *In re Rahrer*[34] was decided the commerce power was being quite uniformly treated as an exclusive power, and the regulation of original package sales as within its scope. It was not unreasonable to view the Wilson Act as conferring that power upon the states in the case of intoxicants; that is, granting them a right to exercise part of an exclusively federal power. The Court met this difficulty by a rather ingenious argument substantially as follows. Since the matter is one within the federal commerce power, the silence of Congress would operate to exclude states from its regulation. Action by Congress is no less potent than its silence. Its action in removing "an impediment to the enforcement of the state laws in respect to imported packages in their original condition, created by the absence of a specific utterance on its part" does not delegate any federal powers to the states. The Wilson Act was viewed as merely divesting intoxicants of their character as subjects of

33. At p. 318 of 12 How.
34. (1891) 140 U.S. 545. See also Clark Distilling Co. v. Western Maryland R. Co., (1917) 242 U.S. 311, and United States v. Hill, (1919) 248 U.S. 420, which sustained the Webb-Kenyon Act, and the Reed Amendment thereto, as valid exercises of the federal commerce power. Those Acts involved limited denials of the use of the channels of interstate commerce to intoxicants. See also Chapter III, *infra*.

interstate commerce "at an earlier period of time than would otherwise be the case." The same technique was later used to protect the economic interests of a state, as it conceived those interests, against injury from competition by prision-made goods.[35] Whatever the theory invoked to sustain it, it was a device for expanding the operative effect of state laws governing transactions within them. The limits of its availability have never been precisely defined. It was only recently that the Supreme Court upheld its use to protect the taxing power of the states.[36]

The principles formulated by Chief Justice Marshall in *McCulloch v. Maryland* furnished a favorable basis for a broad expansion of federal powers in general. His opinion in *Gibbons v. Ogden* performed the same function for the commerce power. Its scope is defined by reference to the "genius and character of the whole government" which seems "to be, that its action is to be applied to all the external concerns of the nation, and to those internal concerns which affect the States generally; but not to those which are completely within a particular State, which do not affect other States, and with which it is not necessary to interfere, for the purpose of executing some of the general powers of the government." This language, though applied to federal powers generally, states his theory of the scope of the commerce power as well. Equally comprehensive was his view as to the scope of the power to regulate. It is defined as the power "to prescribe the rule by which commerce is to

35. Whitfield v. Ohio, (1936) 297 U.S. 431.
36. Prudential Ins. Co. v. Benjamin, (1946) 328 U.S. 408.
See also Chapter III, *infra*

be governed," and, "like all others vested in Congress, is complete in itself, may be exercised to its utmost extent, and acknowledges no limitations, other than are prescribed in the constitution . . . the power over commerce with foreign nations, and among the several States, is vested in Congress as absolutely as it would be in a single government, having in its constitution the same restrictions on the exercise of the power as are found in the constitution of the United States."

It remained for his successors on the Court to develop the implications of these premises. The conditions in the nation in his time did not call for any extensive exercise of the commerce power by Congress. It did enact legislation regulating navigation, providing for the construction of interstate highways, and imposing protective tariffs against foreign imports. During the Civil War, and for some time thereafter, it chartered corporations for the construction of railroads. The beginning of its active interposition to regulate the nation's economic life dates from the eighties of the last century. This was in no small measure due to evils that had arisen with which the individual states were unable to cope. Their inability was due in part to the restraints imposed on them by the commerce clause as construed by the Supreme Court. The most important laws enacted in these early stages of what proved to be a permanent movement were the Interstate Commerce Act of 1887 and the Sherman Anti-Trust Act of 1890. The former dealt directly with interstate transportation; the latter sought to protect the then existing national market against the evils of monopoly by prohibiting contracts in restraint of, or aiming to monopolize, interstate trade.

That Congress possessed the power to regulate interstate transportation in some respects had never been denied since *Gibbons v. Ogden*. The Act of 1887 marked the beginning of a federal program for the regulation of interstate carriers that was far advanced by 1933. No difficulty was found in sustaining laws regulating the operating conditions of railroads, their relations to patrons, the rates that might be charged, and the relations between carriers in connection with through routes and joint rates. The basic justification for such measures was that they protected interstate traffic against unreasonable burdens. That the commerce power could be used to promote the growth of interstate commerce and control it with an eye to the welfare not only of those immediately concerned but also of the general public was expressly affirmed in the *Recapture Clause Case*.[37] Attempts at regulating the labor relations of interstate railroads were held invalid at first in *Adair v. United States*.[38] The statute involved made it a misdemeanor for any agent of an interstate railroad to discharge any employee engaged in train operations because of his union membership. The majority of the Court found that there was no such real and substantial relation between interstate commerce and union membership as would warrant such statute. The requisite connection was found to exist when the Court sustained the Second Federal Employer's Liability Act,[39] and the provisions of the Railway Labor Act of 1926 protecting the right of employees to select their own collective bar-

37. Dayton-Goose Creek Ry. Co. v. United States, (1924) 263 U.S. 456.
38. (1908) 208 U.S. 161.
39. Second Employers' Liability Cases, (1912) 223 U.S. 1.

gaining agent without interference from the employer.[40] Congress was admitted to have the power to recognize and protect the right of the employees to organize. This represented a marked change in attitude from that revealed in the *Adair Case*.

In none of the cases involving Congressional control over labor relations was the position taken that they were interstate commerce. The test of Congress' power to regulate was their relation to the protection or promotion of that commerce and the public interest in freeing it from obstructions. Considerations of the same general type ultimately led to sustaining the Sherman Anti-Trust Act where the conduct involved was not interstate commerce but a contract for the purpose of stifling competition in interstate trade.[41] The Court rejected the contention that the commerce clause gave Congress no power to regulate private contracts, except in the case of public carriers, even though their purpose and effect was to injure interstate commerce. The decisions in *Stafford v. Wallace*[42] and *Chicago Board of Trade v. Olson*,[43] sustaining the Packers and Stockyards Act of 1921 and the Grain Futures Act of 1922, were mere applications of the same principles to transactions no less closely connected with interstate commerce than the contracts involved in *Addyston Pipe & Steel Company v. United States*.[44] Some of the regulated transactions and activities were described as being in

40. Texas & N.O. R. Co. v. Brotherhood of Ry. & S.S. Clerks, (1930) 281 U.S. 548.

41. Addyston Pipe & Steel Co. v. U.S., (1899) 175 U.S. 211. See also Northern Securities Co .v. U.S., (1904) 193 U.S. 197.

42. (1922) 258 U.S. 495.

43. (1923) 262 U.S. 1.

44. (1899) 175 U.S. 211.

the current of interstate commerce; the purely intrastate character of others of them was admitted. Regulation of the former could be upheld because the activities were a part of interstate commerce; control of the latter, because of their close relation to such commerce. A case involving a much more sweeping assertion of federal power was *Railroad Commission of Wisconsin v. C. B. & Q. R. Co.*[45] A provision of the Transportation Act of 1920 empowered the Interstate Commerce Commission to remove unreasonable discriminations against interstate commerce. It exercised this power by prescribing rates for intrastate transportation after finding that existing rates fixed by state authority unreasonably discriminated against it. The provision of the Act conferring that power was held a proper exercise of the commerce power. It did no more than extend somewhat the principle stated by Mr. Justice Hughes in the *Minnesota Rate Cases*[46] that "the execution by Congress of its constitutional power to regulate interstate commerce is not limited by the fact that intrastate transactions may have become so interwoven therewith that the effective government of the former incidentally controls the latter." This conclusion was said to result necessarily "from the supremacy of the national power within its appointed sphere." Prescribing rates for intrastate traffic can scarcely be considered as incidental control of local commerce. It is apparent that by 1933 the Court had fashioned important instruments for the

45. (1922) 257 U.S. 563.
46. (1913) 230 U.S. 352. For further cases in the history of the development of federal control over intrastate railroad rates, see Houston E. & W. T. R. Co. v. U. S., (1914) 234 U.S. 342; American Express Co. v. South Dakota, (1917) 244 U.S. 617; New York v. U.S., (1922) 257 U.S. 591.

control and regulation of local matters so far as that was necessary to foster or protect interstate commerce, whether that consisted of interstate transportation or interstate commercial intercourse.

It was recognized from the time when the commerce clause received its first extensive consideration that interstate commerce did not "comprehend that commerce . . . which does not extend to or affect other States." This idea has furnished the basis for persistent attacks upon the expansion of the federal commerce power. It has been frequently combined with an appeal to the Tenth Amendment. The core of these objections was that Congress was either directly or indirectly regulating, or attempting to regulate, a matter whose control lay within the exclusive competence of the states. The development and acceptance of the principles already discussed have greatly narrowed their scope. They retained considerable force when Congressional prohibitions of interstate commerce were involved. The power to prohibit foreign commerce by means of embargoes was admitted in *Gibbons v. Ogden* as a valid exercise of the commerce power. The extent of the power to prohibit interstate commerce, as developed prior to 1933, was a matter of considerable doubt. The cases in which it had been most frequently considered involved prohibitions of interstate transportation. The first case in which it was considered at length was *Champion v. Ames*,[47] involving the validity of the act forbidding the interstate shipping of lottery tickets. The defendant, who had been convicted of its violation, denied that the power to regulate included that of pro-

47. (1903) 188 U.S. 321.

hibition. The act was sustained by a closely divided Court. The theories of Chief Justice Marshall and Justice Johnson in *Gibbons v. Ogden* furnished the majority with its major premises. The language of the former that the power is vested in Congress as absolutely as if vested in a single government, and of the latter that it "amounts to nothing more than a power to limit and restrain it at pleasure" were cited with approval. Since its scope is so broad, Congress may protect the people of all the states by providing that "such commerce shall not be polluted by the carrying of lottery tickets from one State to another." While its major premises and much of its argument would warrant the conclusion that prohibition would be valid in all cases, the majority was not prepared to go that far, and its opinion contained much that indicated that the character of lottery tickets was an important factor in its decision. In subsequent cases the distinction between legitimate and illicit articles of commerce has played an important part in defining the limits of the power to prohibit interstate transportation.[48] The minority defined those limits in terms of the purposes aimed at by the prohibition. If that were regulation of a purely local matter, the prohibition would be outside the federal commerce power. Since the suppression of lotteries belonged to the states, the prohibition against transporting lottery tickets could not be considered as necessary and proper to the execution of the commerce power. Nor may its scope be expanded by reference to current

48. See Hoke v. U.S., (1913) 227 U.S. 308; Clark Distilling Co. v. Western Maryland R. Co., (1917) 242 U.S. 311; Hammer v. Dagenhart, (1918) 247 U.S. 251.

notions of public interest. Thus ran the minority's argument.

The minority's views achieved their final triumph nearly twenty years later in 1918 in *Hammer v. Dagenhart*.[49] The statute involved therein closed the channels of interstate transportation to goods produced in factories in which child labor had been employed within thirty days prior to their removal therefrom. This language suggests that the statute was aimed at goods in whose production child labor had been utilized. One of the grounds for invalidating it closely paralleled that of the minority in *Champion v. Ames*. In substance, it was that, since the production of goods even for the national market was a local matter, the purpose of the statute was to force upon states a federally prescribed policy with respect to child labor in local industry. The regulation thereof was deemed to lie wholly within the state's police power. Congress was held to possess none to require them to exercise it to prevent possible unfair competition among the states. But the case did more than firmly establish the test used by the minority in *Champion v. Ames*. It whittled down the scope of the theory of the majority in that case as well. The device used to accomplish this was to make the character of the prohibited article an important, though probably not a decisive, factor for appraising the validity of a prohibition. Not only was the harmless nature of the article stressed, but prior decisions sustaining prohibitions were distinguished as resting "upon the character

49. (1918) 247 U.S. 251. See H. W. Bikle, "The Commerce Power and Hammer v. Dagenhart," 67 U. of Pa. Law Rev. 21 (1919); E. S. Corwin, "Congress' Power to Prohibit Commerce," 18 Cornell Law Quarterly 477 (1933).

of the particular subjects dealt with and the fact that the scope of governmental authority . . . to prohibit is as to them but the exertion of the power to regulate." The dissent of Justice Holmes was a vigorous attack on this position, and a defense of the thesis that the prohibition was valid because its immediate field of operation was that of interstate commerce. Even the majority admitted that the use of the facilities of interstate commerce could be prohibited to prevent the accomplishment of harmful results. Those in its mind were such as had been present in the cases sustaining prior prohibitions.[50]

The only other important case prior to 1933 was *Brooks v. United States*[51] in 1925. A unanimous Court then held constitutional the Act prohibiting the transportation of stolen automobiles across state lines. The opinion stated that "Congress can certainly regulate interstate commerce to the extent of forbidding and punishing the use of such commerce as an agency to promote immorality, dishonesty or the spread of any evil or harm to the people of other States from the State of origin. In doing this it is merely exercising the police power, for the benefit of the public, within the field of interstate commerce." This was the Court's rationalization of the prior cases sustaining prohibitions. Its manner of distinguishing *Hammer v. Dagenhart* is rather significant. Articles made by child labor were described as harmless, and such as "could be properly transported without injuring any person who either bought or used

50. See Rottschaefer, Handbook of American Constitutional Law, Sec. 140.
51. (1925) 267 U.S. 432.

them." By contrast, the interstate transportation of stolen automobiles was asserted to be a "gross misuse of interstate commerce" which Congress might properly punish "because of its harmful result and its defeat of the property rights of those whose machines" are stolen. The protection of property from theft, except when moving in interstate commerce, is generally considered a function of the states. The stealing of the cars would be a purely local act preceding their transportation across state lines. The intended effect of the statute was to protect such property by making its theft a riskier and less profitable venture. Its purpose was to secure those effects. The prohibition was, therefore, aimed at the protection of an interest whose protection certainly lies within the states' police power. It follows that prohibition might even then be a valid form of regulating interstate commerce if its purpose and effect were the protection of certain local interests deemed legitimate, even though the article involved were itself harmless. It would be difficult accurately to state the law on this subject as it had developed prior to 1933. Interstate transportation could be validly prohibited to prevent it from becoming an agency for the promotion of immorality and dishonesty or for spreading harm from state to state. The harm might result from the nature of goods or persons transported or from the use made of them in the states into which they were being introduced. The emphasis here was on the protection of the interests and local policy of the importing state. However, the "stolen automobile" case recognized that there might be local interests of the state of origin that justified it. But *Hammer v. Dagenhart* required any inferences drawn from applying such tests to be checked by inquiry into purposes of Congress in enacting the prohibition. The confusion that existed was due to the absence of any judicial indication for determining how far the existence of the wrongful purpose was a function of those very factors that tended to establish the validity of this form of regulation. That it might be employed to protect or promote some state policies was clear. That it would be invalid if this were attempted by exerting pressures upon other states with conflicting policies seemed indicated by *Hammer v. Dagenhart*. And, a fortiori, would it have been unconstitutional if used to force upon the states a local policy defined wholly by Congress.

Taxation is one of the most effective forms of regulation. The effects of taxes occur whether or not the legislature intends them. That the primary purpose for conferring the power to tax upon any government is the raising of revenues to defray the costs of government has always been recognized. However, if a government may both regulate and tax a transaction, it may be quite immaterial to which power the financial demand be referable. The situation is different where a government's sole power is to tax it. The federal government is one of delegated and limited powers. There are matters which it may not regulate but may tax. A purported exercise of its taxing power has frequently been assailed as a disguised attempt to regulate a matter beyond its control. In *Veazie Bank v. Fenno*[52] the claim was made that a discriminatory tax on the notes of state banks was "so excessive as to indicate a purpose on the part

52. (1869) 8 Wall. 533.

of Congress to destroy the franchise of the bank," and to be beyond its constitutional power on that account. While it was admitted that the power might be used in an invalid manner "if exercised for ends inconsistent with the limited grants of power in the Constitution," no such abuse was found in that case. Another discriminatory excise came before the Court in *McCray v. United States*.[53] This tax too was claimed to be outside the federal taxing power because aimed at the suppression of oleomargarine colored like butter. No one familiar with the history of the times doubts that to have been its primary purpose. Despite this, the Court stated that "the motive or purpose of Congress" may not be inquired into. Yet less than twenty years later, in 1922, came the decision in the *Child Labor Tax Case*.[54] The financial demand purported to be a special income tax on those who knowingly employed child labor in certain designated industries. The Court said that it would have to be blind not to see that "the so-called tax is imposed to stop the employment of children within the age limits prescribed. Its prohibitory and regulatory effect and purpose are palpable." It was admitted that a tax did not lose its character as such because imposed with an incidental motive of regulation, but its primary aim must be the production of revenue. These were the reasons for holding the exaction not a tax, but a penalty for employing child labor, the regulation of which was then deemed an exclusive state matter. The same reasoning was invoked to invalidate prohibitive taxes on certain transactions on commodity markets, imposed

53. (1904) 195 U.S. 27.
54. (1922) 259 U.S. 20.

as integral parts of an elaborate system of control of such exchanges.[55] While these decisions were definite setbacks to those wishing to use federal taxes as a regulatory device over a wide range of the nation's economic life, the decision in *United States v. Doremus* [56] remained intact despite attempts to have it overruled.[57] There has never been a clearer case of using the federal taxing power for regulating even the local phases of an admitted evil than this. The mere fact that the regulatory features assumed the guise of enforcement machinery for the tax should be immaterial. Rather did it make most evident the purpose to use the tax power primarily for regulating a local matter. Prior to 1933 there had been no Supreme Court decision passing on whether the spending power of the federal government was subject to the same limits as the *Child Labor Tax Case* had applied to its taxing power. Efforts to get a decision thereon had been repelled on wholly different grounds. In practice, federal funds had been expended on many local objects.

The year of 1933 was not that in which occurred the significant changes in the Supreme Court's construction of the Constitution. It did, however, mark the advent to power of an administration whose reform program furnished the Court with the opportunity for launching the modern version of the Constitution. Its early decisions involving the legislation of that program were in the conservative tradition that had characterized its decisions over a long period. This was especially true

55. Hill v. Wallace, (1922) 259 U.S. 44.
56. (1919) 249 U.S. 86.
57. See Linder v. United States, (1925) 268 U.S. 5; United States v. Daugherty, (1926) 269 U.S. 360; Nigro v. United States, (1928) 276 U.S. 332.

where the major issue was the redistribution of power between the nation and the states. The definite turn in direction began in 1937 and has continued ever since. This Chapter has traced the development of the lines of authority that comprised the major tools available to the Court for the performance of its task. It has been almost wholly concerned with those that had been fashioned in dealing with the problem of the extent of federal powers. Those developed for defining the scope of the major constitutional limitations will be considered at appropriate places in the subsequent discussion. The next Chapter will consider the manner in which the Court used the available tools to lay the constitutional basis for the vast expansion of federal powers that has occurred since 1933.

II

The Expansion of Federal Powers since 1933

THE expansion of federal powers that has occured since 1933 has been the result largely of the depression and the war. That due to the former cause is the more important for defining the extent of federal control of our economy in times of peace. That due to the latter is primarily important in relation to the nation's war powers. However, those powers operate in time of peace as well as during war. The decisions defining their extent during a time of actual warfare may reveal principles relevant to determining their peacetime scope. They cannot be ignored in examining how far the Constitution permits federal intervention in the nation's normal social and economic affairs. But the cases arising out of the legislation enacted to meet the depression are the main source of our knowledge as to the present reach of federal powers, and for gauging their probable further expansion and its direction.

The depression had begun with the collapse of a wild orgy of speculation in securities not only on the nation's security exchanges but also through other marketing channels. The resulting fall in security values threatened the solvency of financial institutions. The general deflation of prices intensified these effects. The status of agriculture, which had never recovered completely from the deflation following World War I, aggravated the general situation. Investigations revealed many indefensible financial practices, especially in the public utility field. There holding company had been piled on holding company until the resulting structure had become too complex for comprehension by even those expected to manage it. The concentration of control implicit in such an organization was looked upon as a threat to the public interest. The capital structure was excessive in view of the probable earnings of the operating companies that were relied upon to support it. The most ardent champions of an economy relatively free from government controls recognized as evils many of the results that private enterprise had brought to pass because it had been inadequately regulated. The international political and economic situation was such as prevented a reversal of the trend. This was especially true with respect to prices of our largest export commodities, that is, agricultural products and raw materials generally. The depression endured despite palliatives aimed to restore the imbalance in the domestic and international economy. Its very length not only induced many diverse speculations as to its causes and cure, but also the opportunity for such speculations to take form as definite theories that gained wide acceptance. Practically every one of them called for some form of government action. They differed as to what action was called for by the existing situation. Some called for temporary relief measures only. Others demanded remedies of a more permanent character and of a kind that struck directly at some well-established preconceptions as to the nature of our economic order, the function of government in the economic process, and political theories concerning the nature of our federal system. These cleavages exist today. They are likely to continue as long as the competition between the currently contending social theories and conflicting ideologies endures. The tides of battle may run now in favor of the one, now in favor of the other. The existence of rival social and economic theories means the presence of competing premises from which to derive causal explanations of our ills. The choice of causes is bound to affect the choice of remedies, and thus the character of the legislation enacted. No one today can doubt that the shift in emphasis from individualism to socialism that has occurred within our generation has affected the interpretation of at least some provisions of the Constitution. It is likely to do so in the future. The decisions on the scope of federal power rendered since 1933 can be understood only if these changes in socio-economic theories are taken into account.

Our courts do not habitually break the continuity of the course of their decisions in important fields of law. Precedents are more likely to be overruled by the subtle processes of distinguishing them, limiting them to their facts, or just ignoring them, than by being expressly overruled. Such was the method by which the common law was adapted to changing circumstances and social needs. Such has been the process by which the Constitution has been adapted thereto. It is almost universally recognized that it has been subjected to a rather important reinterpretation since 1933. Though several of the landmark decisions have been explicitly overruled, the greater part of recent changes was effected by adapting accepted principles to changed conditions in which new factors were present that demanded recognition. The vagueness of some of these principles, and the presence of several among which a choice was not unreasonable, greatly facilitated the process. The commerce, taxing, and spending powers of Congress played the leading role in the expansion of federal powers since 1933. It has already been shown that a congeries of principles relating to those powers had been developed by the Supreme Court prior to that date.[1] Their ultimate implications were not wholly consistent. There was nothing compelling the selection of some of them, rather than others, as major premises in particular situations. Not even the principle of federal supremacy imposed any such necessity where the issue was whether a particular exercise of federal power was within the constitutional grant of that power. Despite this, it has at times been an important factor in sustaining Congressional legislation, and was available when the New Deal laws came before the Supreme Court.

There was a rather influential body of opinion that attributed the depression in considerable part to excessive production under the impetus of uncontrolled competition. It was inevitable that any remedial legislation enacted would aim to remove this condition. The National Industrial Recovery Act of 1933[2] was framed on that theory. By its very first section Congress declares the existence of a "national emergency productive

1. See Chapter I.
2. Act of June 16, 1933, Chap. 90, 48 Stat. 195.

of widespread unemployment and disorganization of industry, which burdens interstate and foreign commerce, affects the public welfare, and undermines the standards of living of the American people." This is followed by a statement of national policy that is sufficiently important in connection with the subsequent discussion of other parts of the legislation of this period to justify quoting. It reads:

> "It is hereby declared to be the policy of Congress to remove obstructions to the free flow of interstate and foreign commerce which tend to diminish the amount thereof; and to provide for the general welfare by promoting the organization of industry for the purpose of cooperative action among trade groups, to induce and maintain united action of labor and management under adequate governmental sanctions and supervision, to eliminate unfair competitive practices, to promote the fullest possible utilization of the present productive capacity of industries, to avoid undue restriction of production (except as may be temporarily required), to increase the consumption of industrial and agricultural products by increasing purchasing power, to reduce and relieve unemployment, to improve standards of labor, and otherwise to rehabilitate industry and to conserve natural resources."

This policy was to be carried into execution by means of codes of fair competition promulgated by the President if he found them to impose no inequitable restrictions to admission to the trade or industrial association to which they were to apply, and that they were not designed to oppress small enterprises or promote monopoly. He might either approve codes formulated by the trade or industry, or, under certain conditions, himself prescribe codes. Section 7 of the Act required every code to contain provisions protecting labor's right of collective bargaining and outlawing the "yellow dog" contract. Violation of any provisions of a code after its promulgation was made a punishable offense. Provision was made for participation by the industry to be controlled in devising the system of control. To that extent it had the appearance of self-regulation so far as codes were promulgated on application by industrial groups. However, after its approval, the code constituted the standard of fair competition for the entire trade or industry. It applied to all transactions in or affecting interstate or foreign commerce of every member in the trade or industry, even those who had had no part in initiating the application for the code and though they might be opposed to it. This could hardly be described as self-regulation in their cases. Codes initiated by the President could be put in force only after notice and hearing. They were no more self-regulation of industry than the others were. The underlying theories of this system are reflected in the statement of policy which was quoted above. One was that the depression was due in some measure to the evils of excessive competition. Hence the provision for federal prescription of certain vaguely defined standards of competitive practices. The labor provisions were part of a deliberate policy of promoting the growth of labor unions and the spread of collective bargaining. It was hoped thereby to stabilize the economy and to increase mass purchasing power. The view that the depression was partly caused by its lack had strong support in influential quarters. The reference was usually to money purchasing power. Although this theory played a larger part in shaping certain other legislation of the period, its influence on this part of the National Industrial Recovery Act cannot be ignored.

The enactment of this legislation produced a veritable rash of codes, and a flood of litigation. While the cases in the lower federal courts dealt with a wide variety of code provisions, those involving the regulation of labor relations were the principal subject of consideration by the Supreme Court. This also applies to the Bituminous Coal Conservation Act of 1935.[3] A decision by the Supreme Court involving each of them was not long in coming. The validity of the National Industrial Recovery Act was determined in *A. L. A. Schechter Corporation v. United States.*[4] The defendant was charge with violations of the "Live Poultry Code." The provisions of present interest were those fixing minimum wages and maximum hours for its employees, and requiring those who bought poultry from it to accept the run of any coop as purchased by it, except for culls. It was an important part of the established channel through which New York City received its supply of poultry from extrastate sources. All its sales were purely local. The activities of its employees at its slaughter house, and its local sales, were held not to be transactions in interstate commerce. The attempt of the government to bring them within the scope of federal commerce power by use of the "current of interstate commerce" concept failed utterly. No more successful was its effort to validate these code provisions by resort to the principle

3. Act of August 30, 1935, Chap. 824, Secs. 1-23, 49 Stat. 991.
4. (1935) 295 U.S. 495.

that the commerce power includes the regulation of matters substantially affecting interstate commerce. The hours and wages of the defendant's employees were held matters that affected commerce indirectly only. That they might lower prices if left unregulated, and thus demoralize the price structure, was declared to prove too much, since it would subject to federal control all the manufacturing and distribution costs of local industry. The theory that the regulations were needed to protect states with high standards from the competition of those with lower standards proved inadequate to sustain their validity. The decision on these points limited the value of codes generally. The decision that the entire system involved an invalid delegation to the President of Congress' legislative powers destroyed them completely at a time when they seemed about to expire of their own ineffectiveness. It should be noted that the entire Court, including Justices Stone and Cardozo, agreed that the commerce clause afforded no basis for the regulations in issue.

The following year the Bituminous Coal Conservation Act of 1935 was held invalid so far as it assumed to regulate the labor relations of miners and mine operators.[5] The mining of coal was analogized to local manufacturing. That decision did little more than follow the orthodox views of the commerce clause as the *Schechter Case* had done. The opinion of Justice Sutherland battled as vigorously as ever to reject the theory that was then gaining increasing support, that the power of the federal government inherently extends to purposes affecting the nation as a whole with which the states

5. Carter v. Carter Coal Co., (1936) 298 U.S. 238.

severally cannot deal or cannot adequately deal, and the related notion that Congress, entirely apart from those powers delegated by the Constitution, may enact laws to promote the national general welfare. It proved to be but a rearguard action in a losing battle. But the reversal of the Court's attitude, when it came, was not effected through its adoption of these proscribed views. It was, however, furthered by its refusal to treat the fact that a delegated power was being used for the purpose of promoting that general welfare, in situations where state power was deemed inadequate, as a decisive factor in finding its exercise unconstitutional.

The common element in these two cases was that each held invalid a federal attempt at regulating the relations of employers to employees who were not engaged in interstate or foreign commerce. Between the dates when they were decided the Court had passed on a case involving employers and employees who were engaged in interstate commerce. Congress had enacted the Railroad Retirement Act in 1934.[6] This established a pension system for railroad employees, and provided for a fund to which both employers and employees were required to contribute. The contributions of all carriers and their employees were pooled into a single fund. A majority of the Court denied that the commerce clause warranted legislation of this character.[7] It rejected the claim that the Act would promote the safety and efficiency of interstate transportation, holding it to be an

6. Act of June 27, 1934, Chap. 868, 48 Stat. 1283; U.S.C., Title 45, Chap. 9.

7. Railroad Retirement Bd. v. Alton R.R. Co., (1935) 295 U.S. 330. See T. R. Powell, "Commerce, Pensions, and Codes," 49 Harv. Law Rev. 1, 193 (1935).

"attempt for social ends to impose by sheer fiat non-contractual incidents upon the relation of employer and employee, not as a rule or regulation of commerce and transportation between the States, but as a means of assuring a particular class of employees against old age dependency." It was "neither a necessary nor an appropriate rule or regulation affecting the due fulfilment of the railroads' duty to serve the public in interstate transportation." A reading of the entire opinion leaves it uncertain whether the basis is the particular features of this Act or such as would have invalidated any legislation establishing such a system. It is a point of interest that the ultimate purpose sought was an important factor in the majority's reasoning. The decision is to that extent in line with the approach of *Hammer v. Dagenhart*. A minority of four found the substantial relation of the plan to the protection of interstate commerce that the majority had denied to exist.

When the next important case involving the scope of the commerce power reached the Supreme Court, the controversy concerning the Court Packing Plan had not yet run its course. It was the first of a series of cases extending over several years dealing with the validity of various applications of the National Labor Relations Act of 1935.[8] The declared policy of the Act was to remove obstructions to the flow of interstate and foreign commerce resulting from the denial by employers of their employees' right to organize for purposes of collective bargaining and the protection of their rights

8. Act of July 5, 1935, Chap. 372, 49 Stat. 449; U.S.C., Title 29, Chap. 7. For Railroad Retirement Act of 1937, see Chap. 382, 50 Stat. 307; U.S.C., Title 45, Chap. 9.

generally. It also invoked the theory that the absence of collective bargaining tends to aggravate depressions "by depressing wage rates and the purchasing power of wage earners in industry and by preventing the stabilization of competitive wage rates and working conditions within and between industries." This reflects substantially the same underlying analysis of the depression that led to the enactment of the legislation already discussed. The facts of *National Labor Relations Board v. Jones & Laughlin Steel Corporation*[9] made it an excellent case from the government's point of view. The business of the corporation and its subsidiaries was organized in a single integrated enterprise drawing its raw materials from some states, transporting them to its manufacturing plant located in another, and shipping most of its finished products to points outside the latter. The unfair labor practices with which it was charged involved its production employees. Their position in the total process afforded some basis for analogizing the relation of their activities to interstate commerce to that of the persons whose practices were held subject to federal control in *Stafford v. Wallace* and *Chicago Board of Trade v. Olson*. The analogy was far from perfect, and the Court declined to base its decision on the "stream of commerce" theory, which it described as a metaphor that did not define the full scope of Congress' power over interstate commerce. It rested its decision on the much more fundamental and established principle that the commerce power permitted any legislation appropriate for the protection and promotion of interstate commerce. Burdens upon it may be removed

9. (1937) 301 U.S. 1.

though their source be local when considered apart from their effect upon that commerce. That a strike of workers engaged in local production was sufficiently related to interstate commerce to bring it within the scope of the Sherman Anti-Trust Act had been recognized in the *Second Coronado Case*.[10] Little further reasoning was required to sustain the order entered by the Board as an appropriate means for attaining a permissible objective. That order required the employer to restore employees discharged for union activities to their former employment and awarded them back pay.

This was a far cry from the *Adair Case*. Nor can it be reconciled successfully with *Carter v. Carter Coal Company*, decided the year before. Decisions rendered within a two-year period of the *Jones & Laughlin Steel Corporation Case* effectively negatived the significance of certain adventitious circumstances present in it and which had lightened the Court's task of establishing the requisite relation of the regulated activities to interstate commerce.[11] The source of the raw materials used in the manufacturing process, the absence of interstate sales by the producer, soon became nonessential factors. It is also not of decisive moment that interstate commerce may be affected but slightly in the given case, since the total effects thereon of similar cases may produce far-reaching injury to such commerce. All these had been given some weight in the *Jones & Laughlin*

10. Coronado Coal Co. v. United Mine Workers of America, (1925) 268 U.S. 295.

11. Santa Cruz Fruit Packing Co. v. N.L.R.B., (1938) 303 U.S. 453; Consolidated Edison Co. v. N.L.R.B., (1938) 305 U.S. 197; N.L.R.B. v. Fainblatt, (1939) 306 U.S. 601; N.L.R.B. v. Bradford Dyeing Ass'n, (1940) 310 U.S. 318.

Case. The Act, it was said, would be valid even as applied to an employer not engaged in interstate commerce. Since 1939 attacks upon the validity of its application have been generally of a rather perfunctory character. The case of *Polish National Alliance v. National Labor Relations Board*[12] is an exception. The conduct of an insurance business on a nationwide scale comprised an important part of Alliance's activities. The Act was invoked on behalf of its office employees at the main office in Chicago, and the Board's order granting the relief asked for was upheld. A strike of its employees would have affected interstate commerce much as would a strike of the class of Associated Press employees who had been held entitled to the protection of the Act in the *Associated Press Case*.[13] Had these alone been relied upon, the case would have added little to what had already been decided. But a new factor was added. As an investor in corporate securities Alliance was stated to play a "credit rôle in interstate industries, railroads, and other public utilities." Its financial transactions could not be "impeded even temporarily without affecting to an extent not negligible the interstate enterprises" in which its assets were invested. The control of its labor relations to prevent interference with the normal flow of investment money into industries producing for the interstate market is thus recognized as having a substantial relation to interstate commerce. Its regulation was accordingly held to be within the federal commerce power.

It would be inaccurate to charge the Court with

12. (1944) 322 U.S. 643.
13. The Associated Press v. N.L.R.B., (1937) 301 U.S. 103.

having broken completely with the past in this line of decisions. The principal tool which it used had been developed and employed by it well before 1933. It would be equally erroneous to represent what it did as involving no break with its past. The possibilities of federal expansion increased when these decisions were rendered. This was the very grievance of those Justices who continued their dissents well after the change in direction had become firmly established.[14] The national economy is a vast and extremely complex organism. It had been growing in this direction from the very beginning of the nation's history. The greater its complexity, the easier to discover some relationship among its integral parts that might reasonably be described as substantial. An interference at one point affects what happens within another area of economic activity, and the degree of those effects often varies directly with the complexity of the system. That these facts alone do not compel a change in judicial perspective has been proved. The extent of integration of our economic system had not increased between the decision in the *Schechter Case* and that in the *Jones & Laughlin Case*. The Court had merely become more willing to accept the judgment of Congress, and the agency created to administer its policy, on what activities required regulation for the protection or promotion of interstate commerce. It broadened its own concept of "substantially affecting interstate commerce" by accepting fully the closely integrated character of the national economy as the basic principle in defining its content. The inevitable

14. See the dissenting opinions of Justice Butler in the first three cases cited in note 11, *supra.*

result has been to enhance the opportunities of Congress effectively to promote any national policy if that can be related to interstate or foreign commerce by some real or imagined chain of causation however many links it may contain. No one can reasonably doubt that the National Labor Relations Act had as its principal purpose the fostering of labor unions and of collective bargaining as a general national policy.

An important aim of much of Congressional legislation of the depression period was to change the distribution of income from that determined by the usual operations of the economic system. The numerous statements of policy that became so prominent a feature of this legislation generally used the expression "to increase purchasing power" to describe this objective. Mention has already been made of its presence in the statements of policy found in the National Industrial Recovery Act and the National Labor Relations Act. The fostering of labor unions as a national policy was expected to promote this aim by increasing the chances of raising wage levels. This was also the deliberate purpose of most of the legislation relating to agriculture. The methods most frequently used for achieving higher incomes for particular groups are subsidies and price control. The former may prove too expensive to the taxpayer, and the latter may prove too difficult of successful execution, if supply is left unregulated. Hence the emphasis in programs of this nature on production control. The first effort to secure this, based on the federal taxing and spending powers, failed for reasons that will be discussed fully when considering those powers.[15] The Agri-

15. United States v. Butler, (1936) 297 U.S. 1. See *infra*, pp. 80–87.

cultural Marketing Agreement Act,[16] based on the commerce power, fared better at the Court's hands. An order issued thereunder by the Secretary of Agriculture established an elaborate system for marketing milk in the New York City milk shed. It prescribed minimum prices to be paid producers by handlers, and provided an equalization pool intended to insure the former uniform prices. The attacks on these features invoked several constitutional provisions, but for the moment only that based on the commerce clause is relevant. The power of Congress to fix prices for interstate sales had been left undecided in the *Carter Coal Company Case*. The four Justices who had expressed themselves on the issue had supported it. The issue was definitely decided in favor of Congress' power in *United States v. Rock Royal Co-Operative, Inc.*[17] The extent of its power in this respect can be gathered from the statement in the prevailing opinion that "The power enjoyed by the states to regulate the prices for handling and selling commodities within their internal commerce rests with the Congress in the commerce between the states." There was no dissent from this proposition. The power to regulate prices of interstate sales of coal was unanimously sustained in the succeeding term of Court.[18] It extends also to fixing prices for wholly intrastate sales in an area in which interstate sales are being thus controlled.[19] Federal power to regulate intrastate transactions is not limited to those "engaged also in interstate

16. Act of June 3, 1937, Chap. 296, 50 Stat. 246; U.S.C., Title 7, Chaps. 26 and 26A.
17. (1939) 307 U.S. 533.
18. Sunshine Anthracite Coal Co. v. Adkins, (1940) 310 U.S. 381.
19. United States v. Wrightwood Dairy Co., (1942) 315 U.S. 110.

commerce." The federally established policy may be protected against frustration by the competition of local producers and marketing agencies by any appropriate means. No one could reasonably claim that federal price control of local sales is not an appropriate means for protecting a federally established price policy for the interstate market. The prices involved in all these cases were minimum prices. The power of Congress to establish maximum prices, or maximum and minimum prices, is equally great. Whatever limits the due process clause of the Fifth Amendment may impose upon the exercise of this power need not be considered here. Not only has the scope of the subject matter within the power of Congress to regulate been expanded, but these cases sustain a kind of regulation for such transactions that would have been held beyond its power less than five years before the date of the *Rock Royal Case*. It went well beyond fixing interstate transportation rates, and the charges for services rendered by buyers and sellers of livestock at the stockyards which were being regulated under the Packers and Stockyards Act. A more intensive regulation over a wider area of activities has now become possible.

The control of agricultural production occupied a prominent place in federal attempts to rehabilitate agriculture. The depressed state of that industry had occupied the attention of Congress ever since the deflation of agricultural prices following the close of World War I. The farmer's share in the national income had been continually decreasing. The depression merely aggravated the farmer's plight. Its principal causes were alleged to be the highly competitive nature of the industry, the chronic over-production that afflicted it, and the practices of those engaged in marketing the products in the national and international markets. That which received the most attention when Congress intervened after 1933 was excessive production. The attempt of the federal government to remedy this by a system of subsidies granted those who would cooperate in a federally determined plan for reducing production has already been mentioned. Its collapse, and the need for the cooperation of those who might refuse to participate in a voluntary plan of control, eventuated in legislation that prevented a determined miniorty from hampering the efforts of those who were willing to cooperate on a voluntary basis. The result was the Agricultural Marketing Act of 1938.[20] It authorized the Secretary of Agriculture, upon making certain findings of fact, to proclaim a national marketing quota for a given agricultural commodity which was to be in effect for the subsequent marketing year. It was to be operative unless disapproved by more than one-third of the producers of that crop for the preceding marketing year. The quota, if not thus disapproved, was allocated by an elaborate system aimed at fixing the quota which each individual producer would be permitted to market during the marketing year for which a national quota had been approved. Sales by any producer in excess of his allotted quota were subject to such heavy penalties as to insure that they would be at a loss. The plan applied as well to those who had opposed it as to those who had voted in its favor. It was, accordingly, wholly compulsory as to the former. The first case under it

20. Act of Feb. 16, 1938, Chap. 30, 52 Stat. 31; U.S.C., Title 7, Chap. 35.

involved a tobacco marketing quota. The Act did not purport to control production, but rather the marketing of tobacco in interstate and foreign commerce. Its ultimate purpose was clearly to control production. No intelligent producer would be likely to produce any amount in excess of his marketing quota if the excess could be disposed of only at a loss. Nevertheless, the Court's majority had no difficulty in sustaining the Act as a regulation of commerce.[21] The broad lines along which its argument proceeds is apparent from the following language from the opinion:

> "Any rule, such as that embodied in the Act, which is intended to foster, protect and conserve that commerce, or to prevent the flow of commerce from working harm to the people of the nation, is within the competence of Congress. Within these limits the exercise of the power, the grant being unlimited in its terms, may lawfully extend to the absolute prohibition of such commerce, and *a fortiori* to limitation of the amount of a given commodity which may be transported in such commerce. The motive of Congress in exerting the power is irrelevant to the validity of the legislation."[22]

A dissent by Justice Butler, concurred in by Justice McReynolds, objected that the theory of the prevailing opinion as to the scope of Congress' power to prohibit interstate commerce was contrary to reason and precedent. It relied upon *United States v. Butler* to hold the Act invalid as a regulation of commerce. There was much in the Court's previous decisions and opinions to support this dissent. What the dissent overlooked

21. Mulford v. Smith, (1939) 307 U.S. 38.
22. At p. 48 of 307 U.S.

was the marked changes that had occurred in political and social philosophy. These had prepared the ground for reasoning from other constitutional premises that also were embodied in judicial decisions and opinions.

The majority's theory in *Mulford v. Smith* was in direct contradiction with that applied in *Hammer v. Dagenhart*. It was clear that the latter was on its way out. Its final exit came about two years later when it was explicitly overruled in *United States v. Darby*.[23] The case was a criminal proceeding for violation of several of the provisions of the Fair Labor Standards Act of 1938.[24] The principal aim of that legislation was to raise the standard of living and promote the general welfare of workers employed in designated industries producing for the national market. This was to be accomplished by establishing minimum wage rates and maximum hours for workers engaged in interstate commerce or in the production of goods for interstate commerce. The shipment in such commerce of goods produced in violation of the Act was prohibited. Violations of this prohibition, and of the minimum wage and maximum hour provisions, were made punishable offences. Minimum wage laws by their very nature involve a most direct governmental interposition in the process of distributing the national income. It is but a special case of price fixing. The minimum wage provisions of the Fair Labor Standards Act merely applied to labor a method of regulation that had already been upheld as applied to milk and coal before the *Darby Case* was decided. It is safe to assume that Congress

23. (1941) 312 U.S. 100.
24. Act of June 15, 1938, Chap. 676, 52 Stat. 1060; U.S.C., Title 29, Chap. 8.

thought of these provisions of this Act as another device for increasing purchasing power.

The *Darby Case* involved the validity not only of the minimum wage and maximum hours provisions of the Act, but also of the prohibition against shipping in interstate commerce the goods produced in violation of those provisions. It was in that part of the Court's opinion sustaining this prohibition that *Hammer v. Dagenhart* was expressly overruled and described as "a departure from the principles which have prevailed in the interpretation of the Commerce Clause both before and since the decision," whose vitality, as a precedent, had "long since been exhausted." All attempts to distinguish the many cases in which prohibition had been held a valid form of regulation were cavalierly brushed aside. The Court based its decision on the theory that Congress has practically unlimited power to follow its own conception of public policy in excluding from interstate commerce articles whose use in the state of destination it believes to be injurious to public welfare, even though that state has not regulated their use. The principles used to sustain the conditional exclusion of intoxicants and prison-made goods are thus not definitive of the scope of this power. It is a fair inference from the freedom of Congress to follow its own views of public policy that prohibition would be valid even though it ran counter to the policy of the state of destination. The policy of the Fair Labor Standards Act ran directly counter to the policy of the state of origin of the goods. There is no reason why the policy of the state of destination is entitled to any greater consideration. The *Darby Case* also effectively abolished another theory that had received frequent recognition by the Court. The decision in *Hammer v. Dagenhart* was due to the Court's view that the Child Labor Act invaded the reserved powers of the states because its ultimate purpose, and Congress' motive in enacting it, was to regulate child labor, not to regulate interstate commerce. The Court did find in the instant case that "The motive and purpose of the present regulation are plainly to make effective the Congressional conception of public policy that interstate commerce should not be made the instrument of competition in the distribution of goods produced under substandard labor conditions, which competition is injurious to the commerce and to the states from and to which the commerce flows." Such a motive and purpose are directly related to interstate commerce. The same view might have been taken of the Child Labor Act. However, the *Darby Case* is not concerned to prove that the Court adopted an erroneous view as to the motive and purpose of Congress in enacting the Child Labor Act. It rejects their relevancy in determining the validity of regulations that operate immediately in the field of interstate commerce. "Whatever their motive and purpose, regulations of commerce which do not infringe some constitutional prohibition are within the plenary power conferred on Congress by the Commerce Clause." The "constitutional prohibitions" referred to are such as are found in the due process clause and other constitutional limitations. The commerce clause itself would not be one of these. Since any prohibition of interstate commerce, whether absolute or conditional, by its very terms directly operates within the field of such commerce, no such prohibition will hereafter be held invalid as long as the *Darby Case* remains law. It may be remarked also that the theory that the Tenth Amendment did anything more than make explicit what was already implicit in the Constitution was completely discarded. That Amendment constitutes no independent limitation on any federal powers.

The minimum wage and maximum hours provisions were held valid on two distinct grounds. The first only will be considered at this point. It assumes as a fact that the employer is producing goods which, at the time of their production, he intends or expects to move in interstate commerce. The intrastate character of the activities of workers engaged in local production is recognized. But the principle defining the power of Congress to regulate local activities received a somewhat different formulation than before. The commerce power is said to extend "to those activities intrastate which so affect interstate commerce or the exercise of the power of Congress over it as to make regulation of them appropriate means to the attainment of a legitimate end, the exercise of the granted power of Congress to regulate interstate commerce." Some indication of its scope can be gleaned from its use in this case. In sustaining the prohibition of interstate commerce already discussed, the unfettered power of Congress to establish the national policy for interstate commerce had been proclaimed. Since it had adopted the policy of excluding goods produced under substandard labor conditions, as defined by the Fair Labor Standards Act, it could choose any means reasonably adapted to making that policy effective. That aim would become easier of attainment the fewer the goods produced under such conditions available for shipment in interstate commerce. It would be completely realized if no goods intended for the national market were produced under such conditions. It was easy to conclude that directly imposing upon producers for the national market the minimum wage and maximum hours standards, and punishing them for failure to observe them, would be an appropriate means for executing the national policy denying the channels of interstate commerce to goods produced under substandard labor conditions. Such is the substance of one line of reasoning followed in sustaining the validity of the wage and hour requirements of the Fair Labor Standards Act. The scope of permissible federal intervention in the nation's productive activities has been greatly expanded by this theory.

The connection between production for the national market and interstate commerce is rather immediate. Its direct regulation might well have been, and in fact was, upheld apart from its relation to the prohibition against transporting in interstate commerce the goods produced under substandard conditions. It had been held frequently that Congress might protect interstate commerce against evils of local origin. A great deal of legislation had been enacted to protect those engaged therein from the unfair trade practices of their competitors. The competition from goods produced under substandard labor conditions had merely to be included among unfair competitive practices to permit Congress to take appropriate protective measures against it. This is substantially the second line of reasoning used to sustain the wage and hour provisions of the Fair Labor Standards Act.

The narrowest possible interpretation of the decision in the *Darby Case* would be that it upheld the power of Congress to deny the use of the channels of interstate commerce for failure to comply with regulations that it could have imposed in any event. It would be the worst kind of self-deception for anyone to expect that its scope will be thus limited. It is a fair question whether there are any limits on Congress' power to fix the conditions on which access may be had to the channels of interstate commerce. With what regulations may it require a person to comply as the price exacted for his use of those channels? The problem arises in an acute form when Congress uses its power over interstate commerce to support federal regulation of a vast business whose activities comprise a congeries of predominantly local transactions interwoven with some that are clearly interstate. The cases that raised this issue most clearly are those involving the Public Utility Holding Company Act of 1935.[25] Its enactment undoubtedly was due to the undeniable abuses of financial power that accompanied the construction during the 1920's of vast holding company systems having no sound economic justification. The collapse of some of these had intensified the financial crisis that inaugurated, but probably did not cause, the depression. The properties controlled by many of them could by no stretch of the imagination be said to constitute an integrated economic unit. There was also a widespread

25. Act of Aug. 26, 1935, Chap. 687, 49 Stat. 838; U.S.C., Title 15, Chap. 2C.

belief that they imposed an unnecessary cost on the operating companies to the detriment of consumers. The provisions of the Act reflect the presence of all of these factors. It regulates their finances, the relation of the holding company and its subsidiaries, the acquisition of operating properties or their control, and confers upon the Securities and Exchange Commission the power to require such simplification of holding company systems as will eliminate use of the device where it cannot be justified on economic grounds. These control provisions apply only to registered holding companies. The penalty for failure to register is the denial to unregistered holding companies of the use of the mails and the channels of interstate commerce in carrying out the numerous activities necessary to the control and management of the system. The same device was employed to force registered holding companies to comply with many of the regulations imposed upon them. It is these that raise the issue of the extent to which Congress may use its power over interstate commerce to regulate intrastate transactions and relations.

The first case to reach the Supreme Court involved only the registration provisions of the Act.[26] The Securities and Exchange Commission had brought proceedings to compel Electric Bond & Share Company and some of its secondary holding companies to comply therewith. The Company conceded that it used the mails and the channels of interstate commerce continuously in controlling and managing its system, and that some of its subsidiaries transmitted electric power across state lines

26. Electric Bond & Share Co. v. Securities and Exchange Commission, (1938) 303 U.S. 419.

as a regular part of their business. The presence of these facts was deemed sufficient to negative the defendants' claim that they were "not engaged in activities within the reach of the congressional power." The Court found no occasion to consider the validity of the major provisions of the Act. Since registered holding companies were required to furnish a rather detailed statement as to their corporate structure and activities, the Court was content to sustain it as an appropriate means for securing for Congress information bearing upon activities within the range of its power. Denial of use of the mails and the channels of interstate commerce were held valid methods to force compliance.

The provisions whose validity was in issue in the two other cases thus far decided by the Supreme Court were much more vital to the execution of the Act's ultimate purposes. Federal intervention to eliminate the evils charged to holding companies in the public utility field would have failed almost completely had they been found to violate the commerce clause. In the *North American Company Case*,[27] that Company had been ordered by the Securities and Exchange Commission to divest itself of the securities owned by it in nearly all the subsidiary companies of its system. The *American Power & Light Company Case*[28] involved a Commission order directing the dissolution of two of the intermediate holding companies in the Electric Bond & Share system. The Court's reasoning follows very nearly the same pattern in these two cases except that con-

27. North American Co. v. Securities and Exchange Commission, (1946) 327 U.S. 686.

28. American Power & Light Co. v. Securities and Exchange Commission, (1946) 329 U.S. 90.

cerned with the specific remedy prescribed by the Commission. The presence of the same two basic facts relied on in the registration case support the power of Congress to subject these companies to some form of regulation. But the opinions in each set forth much more fully than did that in the earlier case the Court's basic theory. Each stresses the economic evils "resulting from uncoordinated and unintegrated public utility holding company systems." Those specifically mentioned include concentration of economic control, inequitable distribution of voting power among the security holders of the system, financially irresponsible management, excessive capitalizations, and resistance to rate decreases. The source of these evils was found in the nature and extent of the securities owned by holding companies and in their very existence when not justified by sound economic reasons. It is through their use of the channels of interstate commerce that these evils are spread until they assume national importance. Congress has the power to prevent those channels from becoming "the means of promoting or spreading evil, whether of a physical, moral or economic nature." It may do so by imposing "relevant conditions and requirements" on those who use those channels and enforce such conditions by their denial to those who fail to comply therewith. But Congress may go further and directly promulgate regulations to destroy an evil "once it is established that the evil concerns or affects commerce in more states than one." Since the means employed by holding companies are evils belonging to that class, Congress may prescribe the divestment of securities and the liquidation of holding companies commanded by the orders issued in these cases. The opinions contain sweeping definitions of the scope of the commerce power. In the *North American Company Case* it is stated that "This broad commerce clause does not operate so as to render the nation powerless to defend itself against economic forces that Congress decrees inimical or destructive of the national economy." In the other the power of Congress under the commerce clause is held to include that of solving national problems "directly and realistically" since that power "is as broad as the economic needs of the nation."

These opinions leave one in doubt as to their import because of the confusing intermingling of what appear to be separate lines of reasoning. One line stresses the power of Congress to prevent the channels of interstate commerce from being used for the promotion or spread of evils. Another follows the traditional lines by which the power of Congress has been extended to the regulation of matters bearing a substantial relation to interstate commerce. This will be analyzed first to establish its relevance to the issues decided. Emphasis is put on the fact that the holding companies in question were engaged in interstate commerce, through their operating subsidiaries. This is said to "accentuate and add materially to the interstate character" of the holding companies, and to make "more inescapable" the conclusion that they bear not only a "highly important relation to interstate commerce and the national economy" but are engaged in interstate commerce. Clearly the interstate commerce here referred to means something other than the use of its channels for managing and controlling their systems. Insofar as the ownership of the securities of system members, or the existence of unnecessary intermediate holding companies therein might affect these interstate activities of their operating subsidiaries, Congress might direct the divestment of such securities and the dissolution of those unnecessary holding companies. This would constitute no more than an application of principles and methods sustained in the *Northern Securities Company Case*,[29] and frequently used in proceedings under the Sherman Anti-Trust Act. But the effects of the holding companies' structure and control upon the interstate activities of their operating subsidiaries played but a negligible part in the Court's reasoning. Nor do its opinions contain any clear or specific indications of how the proscribed practices involved in these cases, and others within the scope of the Act, substantially affected interstate commerce in general. The Court was justified in treating a holding company as engaged in interstate commerce whenever any of its operating subsidiaries distributed power or gas in interstate commerce. There are probably no holding company systems not engaged in interstate commerce in this sense. But the purpose of the Act was not limited to protecting only the consumers of power and gas that had moved across state lines. It envisaged all consumers of such services. The protection of those not using interstate power and gas would be within the commerce power if their protection bore a substantial relation to interstate commerce. The discovery of such relation in the case on nonindustrial users involves an extension of that concept beyond its pre-1933 limits. It may be that their protection is within the commerce power

29. Northern Securities Co. v. U.S., (1904) 193 U.S. 197.

solely because a holding company is directly engaged in interstate commerce, regardless of the magnitude thereof in relation to its total operations. If the interstate and local distribution are so interwoven in such a case that their regulation cannot be conveniently separated, the protection of such consumers could be readily sustained. If this be not the case, their protection merely because the producer was also engaged in interstate commerce would be of doubtful validity as measured by prior standards. This would also involve an expansion of the commerce power.

It is impossible to determine to what extent these decisions rest on either of these bases. There is much to justify the view that they embody an even more expansive conception of the commerce power, viz., the theory that it enables Congress to do anything necessary and proper to defend the nation against "economic forces that Congress decrees inimical or destructive of the national economy." It is described in the *North American Company Case* as "an affirmative power commensurate with the national needs." Expressions of the same tenor appear in the opinion in the *American Power & Light Company Case*. At the conclusion of the discussion of the commerce clause issue it is said therein:

"... we reaffirm once more the constitutional authority resident in Congress by virtue of the commerce clause to undertake to solve national problems directly and realistically, giving due recognition to the scope of state power. That follows from the fact that the federal commerce power is as broad as the economic needs of the nation."[30]

30. At p. 103 of 329. U. S.

These are broad statements, and nothing in their contexts suggests any principle for limiting their implications. The theory implicit in them is that, if Congress believes the nation's economic welfare to require the adoption and execution of a particular policy, it may use its commerce power to effectuate that policy on a national scale even though the immediate incidence of the regulation is outside the field of interstate commerce itself, and the ultimate objective bear a rather remote connection to that field. The reasons and motives inducing Congress to employ its powers in this manner and for such purpose become wholly immaterial. The statement of policy in the Public Utility Holding Company Act mentions the fact that effective state regulation of public utilities has been made difficult, if not impossible, because the activities of holding companies extended over many states. It may be assumed that this factor contributed to the passage of this Act, and that the Court was well aware of that fact. Nevertheless, there is no reason for believing that its decisions intended to accept the view urged by the government, and rejected by the majority of the Court in the *Carter Coal Company Case*, that the inability of the states to deal, or adequately deal, with a problem affecting the nation at large was a sufficient basis for the exertion of federal powers. While the majority opinion in *United States v. South-Eastern Underwriters Association*[31] had referred to the commerce power as one "to govern affairs which the individual states, with their limited territorial jurisdictions, are not fully capable of governing," the

31. (1944) 322 U.S. 533. See T. R. Powell, "Insurance as Commerce in Constitution and Statute," 57 Harv. Law Rev. 937 (1944).

context indubitably shows that it had in mind only transactions "reaching across state boundaries" and affecting "the people of more states than one." The same idea occurs in these *Public Utility Holding Company Act Cases*, and is but a modern version of that expressed by Chief Justice Marshall in *Gibbons v. Ogden* and frequently repeated thereafter. It seems a fair inference that the broad language already quoted will be limited by the requirement that the economic activities that create a national problem will have to involve some transactions across state lines and affecting the people of more states than one. Even as applied in these cases, the commerce clause is no grant of power to regulate generally to promote the national welfare apart from the presence of some interstate commerce transactions through whose control that welfare may be advanced.

The last statement leads directly into the other line of reasoning supporting these decisions. It concerns the method devised to enforce the policy and general regulatory provisions of the Act. The device was no more novel than the principle from which proceeded the argument in support of its use. It consisted in denying the use of the mails and the channels of interstate commerce to compel both registration and compliance by registered holding companies with the broad and intensive system of regulation to which the Act subjected them.

The power of Congress to deny the use of the channels of interstate commerce to promote a national policy with respect to such commerce had already been established in the *Darby Case* when these *Public Utility Holding Company Act Cases* were decided. It was certain that the application of the same technique to the holding companies would be sustained, and it has been upheld in every case under the Act that has thus far been decided by the Supreme Court. The line of reasoning employed in the *Holding Company Act Cases* to sustain the prohibitions of the Holding Company Act introduced features not found in the reasoning in the *Darby Case*. These dealt with the extent to which Congress may impose conditions that have to be complied with to secure access to the channels of interstate commerce. This problem was inevitably present in the *Darby Case* also, but the legislation involved in it did not as readily suggest it as did that involved in the *Holding Company Act Cases*. That by its very terms conditioned the right to use the channels of interstate commerce upon compliance with its various regulatory provisions. The reasoning of the Court to support its conclusion that the prohibition was valid may be summarized as follows. Its major premise is that Congress has undoubted power under the commerce clause to impose relevant conditions and requirements on those who use the channels of interstate commerce so that those channels will not become conduits for promoting or perpetuating economic evils. Its minor premise is that holding companies in the public utility field use those channels for that purpose and with that result. This is supported by a wealth of factual data which the opinions set forth in general terms. From these premises is drawn the conclusion that Congress may "to the extent that corporate business is transacted through such channels, affecting commerce in more states than one," act directly to protect "what it conceives to be the national welfare" and "prescribe appropriate regulations and determine the conditions under which that business may be pursued."

The opinions of the Court in these cases do not furnish a very satisfactory basis for determining the extent of the regulations with which Congress may require compliance to entitle one to use the channels of interstate commerce for business purposes. They state that the conditions must be "relevant," but do not indicate to what they must be relevant. It may be that the Court meant no more than that the regulations must be such as are appropriate for the protection or promotion of an objective within the scope of the commerce power. This would include the regulation of interstate transactions and of those matters substantially affecting interstate commerce or its regulation. But these may be directly regulated under well established principles. So far as such regulations are concerned, the denial of access to the channels of interstate commerce is merely a means to an end, a particular device for enforcing regulations valid apart from the prohibitory legislation. However, assume that the subject-matter of the regulation is neither an interstate transaction, nor one substantially affecting interstate commerce, and that the business to which it pertains uses the channels of interstate commerce in connection with some of its other transactions. Could Congress deny the use of the facilities of interstate commerce with respect to those latter unless that business complied with federal regulation of the former? The broad scope of the commerce power under recent expansions of the concept "substantially affecting interstate commerce" make it unlikely that cases of this type will occur very often. The *Holding Company Act Cases* give no answer to the question. Their really significant aspect is not that they permit the power to prohibit interstate commerce to be used as a means for enforcing other valid regulations under the commerce power. It is that they sustained the particular regulations in issue on the basis of reasoning that would validate most of the broad controls that have to be complied with to entitle the holding companies to use the mails and the channels of interstate commerce for conducting their operations. These cases differed from the *Darby Case* only in that the connection between the regulated transactions and interstate commerce in it was more immediate than in them, although not so easily sustainable on the basis of the authorities prior to 1933.

It remained for *Wickard v. Filburn*[32] to develop some of the most startling implications of this expansion of the federal commerce power. An acreage allotment for growing wheat for the marketing year had been duly approved in accordance with the provisions of the Agricultural Adjustment Act. Filburn had planted an acreage exceeding his allotment. He generally used the wheat grown on this excess acreage for feeding his livestock and poultry, some of which he marketed, for making flour for home use, and as seed grain. There was no finding as to his intended use of the wheat involved in the case. The effect of the Act was that he could neither dispose of this wheat nor use it for any of those purposes except upon payment of a very severe penalty. This could be avoided only by storing it or delivering it to the Secretary of Agriculture. He sought to enjoin

32. (1942) 317 U.S. 111.

the enforcement of those provisions of the Act that operated in this manner.

The Court immediately recognized that something more than its decision in the *Darby Case* would be required to dispose of this one since these provisions extended federal regulation to production not intended in any part for the national market but wholly for consumption on the farm. However, it had no difficulty in finding a basis for sustaining this extension. Filburn's main contention was that the Act regulated production and consumption, that these were local matters having at most an indirect effect upon interstate commerce, and that the commerce clause furnished no basis for their regulation. Not only was it rejected as an unwarranted reliance upon mechanical applications of legal formulas, its underlying theory was completely demolished by an historical survey of the early development of the commerce power and its expansion after Congress began to use it in an affirmative manner in response to national economic needs. It will be futile hereafter to frame an argument in terms of "direct" or "indirect" effect of local activities upon interstate commerce. The decisive factor is whether they bear a substantial relation to that commerce or to a policy which Congress may adopt with respect thereto. The restrictions imposed by the Act upon production and consumption satisfactorily met this test. The wheat problem, in both its national and international aspects, is analyzed to show the effects of the home consumption of wheat upon the demand for that part of the supply offered for sale or exchange. It was recognized that the Act aimed at raising the price of wheat in the national market by both controlling its supply and increasing the demand for the wheat produced for that market by preventing a person from producing it to meet his own needs. The objective is one that Congress may promote by exercising its commerce power, and those means are appropriate for its realization. It could do so directly by fixing prices for interstate sales of wheat, a power already sustained in the case of milk and coal. But whatever the method it adopt, it may employ means appropriate to making its policy effective. The production of wheat for use on the farm might endanger its success by operating as a threat to that produced for the national market if price rises should induce it to flow into that market. The removal of this threat would warrant resort to methods insuring that it would not reach the market. But this would scarcely justify prohibiting the producer from using it on his own farm. The reasons urged to support this were formulated by the Court in the following language:

> "But if we assume that it is never marketed, it supplies a need of the man who grew it which would otherwise be reflected by purchases in the open market. Home-grown wheat in this sense competes with wheat in commerce. The stimulation of commerce is a use of the regulatory function quite as definitely as prohibitions or restrictions thereon. This record leaves us in no doubt that Congress may properly have considered that wheat consumed on the farm where grown, if wholly outside the scheme of regulation, would have a substantial effect in defeating and obstructing its purpose to stimulate trade therein at increased prices."[33]

33. At pp. 128 and 129 of 317 U.S.

It is quite probable that it would stimulate interstate trade in wheat at increasing prices, but many may doubt its efficacy to stimulate interstate commerce in general, not to mention doing so at increasing prices. That it forced Filburn and those similarly situated to provide a market for what others grew at least is certain. His objection on that score was cavalierly disposed of as a rather usual incident of regulation. The choice between competing economic interests was held a legislative, not a judicial, function. The implications of this decision are enormously important. The point of immediate interest is that the principal tool employed was the familiar concept "substantially affecting interstate commerce." This accords with the technique used in the other decisions that have helped make the commerce power the most important instrument for centralizing control over the national economy in the federal government. The decision still leaves open the question whether Congress may condition the right to use the channels of interstate commerce upon compliance with regulations of matters so purely local as not to come within the broadened scope of the concept mentioned above. It reasonably may be claimed that this question has been deprived of all possible content by this decision.

The commerce power extends to the development of the navigable waters of the United States and the control of navigation thereon. Recent developments in this field have given secondary importance to improving and controlling navigation. The principal objective of much of the legislation relating to these navigable waters has been concerned with the development of the national water power resources. The federal government had for more than a century constructed dams in the navigable waters of the United States in order to improve navigation. It had been held even before 1933 that "the fact that purposes other than navigation will also be served" by a dam would not invalidate its construction "even if those other purposes would not alone have justified an exercise of Congressional power."[34] Its control over the construction of dams by others was equally broad. The power to improve and control navigations was limited to the navigable waters of the United States. The generally accepted definition thereof was waters navigable in fact, used or "susceptible of being used, in their ordinary condition," either alone or in conjunction with other connecting navigable waters, as an avenue of interstate or foreign commerce. This definition dated back to 1871.[35] It was recognized that Congress had the power to control the nonnavigable tributaries of a navigable river so far as that was appropriate to exercising its control over that river. Nevertheless, the old conception of "navigable waters of the United States" imposed some limits on its powers. Its function as a limiting factor has now lost much of its force by its redefinition.

This problem received its most thorough consideration in *United States v. Appalachian Electric Power Company*.[36] This was a suit by the United States to enjoin the Power Company from constructing a power dam in the New River, a tributary of a navigable river

34. Arizona v. California, (1931) 283 U.S. 423.
35. The Daniel Ball, (1871) 10 Wall. 557.
36. (1940) 311 U.S. 377.

of the United States, unless it procured a license from the Federal Power Commission. It had refused to do this because of objections to several of its terms. Some of these were predicated on the theory that the New River was nonnavigable; others were based on considerations applicable even if it were navigable. The issue of its navigability was thus necessarily involved. The view that this was to be decided on the basis of a river's ordinary condition apart from improvements was definitely rejected. It is not necessary that the improvements that would make it navigable be actually completed or even authorized. It suffices that a river be capable of being made navigable by making them. The only limit suggested is that they be reasonable. The only test thereof is framed by the Court in terms of a balance between their cost and the need for them at the time when the improvements "would be useful." In practice this is likely to prove no limit at all. The application of such a test would plunge the Court into questions as difficult as those presented by the rate base problem in the field of public utility regulation. This theory confers upon Congress an effective instrument for defining the scope of its own powers in exercising this part of its commerce power.

The significance of this appears more fully in the Court's reasoning sustaining the validity of the license terms to which the Power Company had objected. These required it to amortize its investment in accordance with a federally prescribed plan, authorized the United States to expropriate excessive profits, and gave the government the right to acquire the company's property, when the license expired, for a price which was

alleged to be so confiscatory as to violate the due process clause of the Fifth Amendment. The Court agreed
with the Company that these provisions were not
essential to or even concerned with navigation as such.
It denied the latter's basic assumption that the federal
government's constitutional power over the navigable
waters of the United States was limited to improving
and controlling navigation thereon. Its scope is measured by the needs of commerce, and includes flood
protection, watershed development, and recovery of
the cost of improvements through the use of the power
developed. The terms to which the Company objected
are thus held to have an obvious relation to the exercise
of the commerce power. Moreover, they would be valid
even though they bore no such relation thereto. Congress' power over the nation's navigable water would
justify it in absolutely prohibiting the construction of
dams therein. Since it could prohibit absolutely, it may
grant its consent on any terms whatever. Submission
to such conditions is the price the Company must pay
for the right to construct and maintain its dam, even
though this involve results that otherwise would violate
the Fifth Amendment. This is a sweeping recognition
that the navigable waters of the United States are subject to national planning and control in more ways
than by merely improving them and regulating traffic
thereon. That Congress may exercise the same powers
with respect to the nonnavigable portions of a stream
navigable in some of its parts, and with respect to the
entire basin of the stream, was held in another case decided in the same term of Court in which the *Appala-*

chian Power Company Case was decided.[37] The exercise of these broad powers, in combination with the power of disposing of the property of the United States, has laid the constitutional basis for embarking on vast programs for the development of power and its distribution. There can be no serious question as to the validity of federal ownership and operation of such an enterprise after *Ashwander v. T.V.A.*[38] That it could use this power to encourage municipal ownership to supplant private ownership of some of our important public utilities was definitely established in *United States v. City and County of San Francisco.*[39] Truly the federal government has been transformed into a powerful instrument for controlling the national economy.

The taxing and spending powers are the other two federal powers that have recently been most relied upon by Congress to achieve social and economic reforms. Both are capable of use as regulatory devices. Both are important instruments for redistributing wealth and current and future national income. The use of the taxing power for purposes of regulation will generally affect the distribution of wealth and income to some extent. This does not prevent separate treatment of taxation as a regulatory device. The Court had sustained Congress' use of this power for that purpose in several cases prior to 1933.[40] But it had also invalidated several statutes, where it found the dominant purpose to be not revenue but the regulation of matters within the exclusive con-

37. Oklahoma v. G. F. Atkinson Co., (1941) 313 U.S. 508.
38. (1936) 297 U.S. 288.
39. (1940) 310 U.S. 16.
40. Veazie Bank v. Fenno, (1869) 8 Wall. 533; McCray v. U.S., (1904) 195 U.S. 27.

trol of the states.[41] This was the basis of the *Child Labor Tax Cases* in which the invalid purpose appeared on the face of the statute. The same line of reasoning led to invalidating a federal excise on producers and vendors of intoxicants carrying on such businesses in any state in violation of its laws.[42] The statute imposing it had been enacted in 1926 while the Eighteenth Amendment was in force. Repeal of the Amendment prevented the levy from being viewed as a measure for its enforcement. Hence, the case was decided on the basis of principles that would have applied had that Amendment never been adopted. So viewed, the imposition was held to be a penalty for violation of state laws, and the taxing act invalid because its purpose was to usurp the states' police powers. The majority's contention that this invalid purpose appeared on the face of the statute was denied by a minority that used some rather tenuous arguments to discover a relation of the statute's provisions to the taxing power. This case was decided a short time before *United States v. Butler*.[43] That was the last in which what purported to be an exercise of the federal taxing power was declared invalid because of its ultimate purpose. In it the regulation of matters then deemed to be within the exclusive control of the states was to be effected not by the mere levy of the tax but by the expenditure of its proceeds. This was held not to affect the application of the principle. Within a little more than a year after its decision the Court sus-

41. Hill v. Wallace, (1922) 259 U.S. 44; Child Labor Tax Case, (1922) 259 U.S. 20.
42. U.S. v. Constantine, (1935) 296 U.S. 287.
43. (1936) 297 U.S. 1.

tained the federal license tax on dealers in firearms.[44] This term was so defined as to include only those selling firearms of the kind usually used by gangsters. It was an integral part of a system of taxes and regulations whose purpose was undoubtedly curbing the sale of such weapons. The principal regulatory provisions did not apply to the particular tax sustained. There were adequate precedents to support the decision. It merely gave actual effect to the frequently asserted principle that the Court could not inquire into the hidden motives of Congress in imposing the tax. The line between such motives which do not affect the validity of a tax, and the ulterior purposes aimed at which condemn it, has always been a difficult one to draw. It may be taken for granted that henceforth Congress will be permitted to use its taxing power as a regulatory device with little, if any, danger that the tax will be held bad because its purpose is to regulate matters which it might not otherwise control.

The point of the objection in most of the cases just considered was that the federal government was invading the reserved powers of the states by regulating matters whose regulation was claimed to lie with the states exclusively. A somewhat different, but related, attack was made on the tax provisions of the Social Security Act.[45] It was claimed that the unemployment insurance tax, and the credit against it for similar taxes paid to a state under an act approved by the federal Social Security Board, coerced the states and destroyed their autonomy. The objection was disposed of in *C. C. Stew-*

44. Sonzinsky v. U.S., (1937) 300 U.S. 506.
45. Act of Aug. 14, 1935, Chap. 531, 49 Stat. 620; U.S.C., Title 42, Chap. 7.

ard Machine Company v. Davis.[46] It was denied that the state, whose taxes the Company would be entitled to credit against its federal tax, had been coerced in enacting its state unemployment insurance act and the tax imposed thereby. However, the decision on this point rests on something more fundamental than that. The national scope and character of widespread unemployment and its attendant evils was held to justify not only using the federal taxing power to alleviate its consequences but also to provide a system enlisting the cooperation of the states to that end. Congress may offer inducements to secure that cooperation. The credit device was justified as a reasonable means for making the plan effective and to prevent duplicated taxation by nation and state, and held to involve no coercion of the states.

The opinion refers to a similar credit provision found in the Federal Estate Tax Act against which the same objection had been made without success. There is a marked difference between this credit and that found in the Unemployment Insurance Act. The Estate Tax Act contains no provision conditioning the taxpayer's right to take it other than payment of the state tax. The state inheritance tax act under which he pays it does not have to be approved by any federal authority. Such approval of the state unemployment insurance act is a condition to the allowance of the credit under the Federal Social Security Act. That this involves the possibility of federal control over state policy far more extensive than that possible under the Estate Tax Act is obvious. If there are no limits on the conditions that

46. (1937) 301 U.S. 548.

Congress may impose, it could in fact subject the states to a most effective coercion with respect to the exercise of any of their powers. The states' freedom of action could become a pure fiction. The possibilities of expanding the scope of federal powers would have been immeasurably enhanced. The Court was fully aware of this problem, and entered the following caveat:

"In ruling as we do, we leave many questions open. We do not say that a tax is valid, when imposed by act of Congress, if it is laid upon the condition that a state may escape its operation through the adoption of a statute unrelated in subject matter to activities fairly within the scope of national policy and power. No such question is before us. . . . It is one thing to impose a tax dependent upon the conduct of the taxpayers, or of the state in which they live, where the conduct to be stimulated or discouraged is unrelated to the fiscal need subserved by the tax in its normal operation, or to any other end legitimately national. . . . It is quite another thing to say that a tax will be abated upon the doing of an act that will satisfy the fiscal need, the tax and the alternative being approximate equivalents. In such circumstances, if in no others, inducement or persuasion does not go beyond the bounds of power. We do not fix the outermost line. Enough for present purposes that wherever the line may be, this statute is within it. Definition more precise must abide the wisdom of the future."[47]

This language does not affirm that there are any such limits. Nor does it logically imply that the Court believes any to exist. But at least it admits the possibility of there being some. It even indicates possible factors relevant to the determination of any there may be. They are certain to be defined in terms so broad as in practice

47. At pp. 590 and 591 of 301 U.S.

to impose few restrictions on Congress in the use of this and similar devices. The opinion might be construed to imply that the method might be availed of to stimulate or discourage conduct related to "the fiscal need subserved by the tax in its normal operation" or related to "any other end legitimately national." The Court has rid itself of the "ulterior purpose" doctrine in defining the scope of the federal taxing power. By suggesting the possibility of another and even vaguer limit, it has created for itself a new series of problems. These can be avoided if it will but deny the existence of any limit of the character suggested by it. It is doubtful that it will choose that solution for a long time to come.

The public benefits derived from taxation are generally secured through the expenditure of the revenues collected. The Constitution authorizes Congress to "lay and collect Taxes ... to ... provide for the common Defense and general Welfare of the United States." Whatever criticisms may have been leveled at *United States v. Butler*, it at least resolved one dispute of long standing when it held that the power to tax for the general welfare authorized Congress to tax, and to expend public moneys, to promote that welfare by financing federal activities that could not be said to be included in the other grants of power to it. The taxing and spending powers can thus be employed independently of any other powers to promote the national welfare. It is merely a matter of showing that the activities being financed by public moneys are promoting the general, as distinguished from the particular, welfare. The taxes levied to defray the costs of the Social Security program were easily held to meet this test. Few would quarrel with that result. As is true with respect to the question of what constitutes a valid public purpose for which the states may tax without violating the due process clause of the Fourteenth Amendment, the question is primarily one for the legislature. Its decision will be set aside only upon a showing that its choice is clearly wrong. In practice this means that the Court will accept the judgment of Congress on this matter as final in almost any conceivable case. The limits on the power to borrow are no greater. Hence, if tax revenues prove inadequate, funds may be borrowed. It is well known to all that the federal government has used these powers to finance relief, to subsidize agriculture and low-cost housing, and to make loans to both private and public agencies for various purposes. While the *Butler Case* did apply to federal spending the same limit imposed upon the taxing power when it was decided, the *Social Security Tax Cases* have in effect overruled it. However, the question may still be considered open how far Congress may impose conditions in making grants of federal moneys to promote the general welfare.[48] It certainly may require compliance with any conditions reasonably adapted to attain the end which justifies the expenditure. This was the position of Justice Stone in his dissent in the *Butler Case*, and it can now be accepted as law. How much further Congress may go in this respect is a matter for the future. The limits mentioned by Justice Stone are sufficient to permit a vast expansion

48. See in this connection Oklahoma v. United States Civil Service Comission, (1947) 330 U.S. 127, 67 S. Ct. 544. This sustained a provision of the Hatch Act requiring a reduction in the amount of a federal grant in aid to the state if the state failed to suspend a state official found to have violated the provisions of that Act.

of federal regulatory power. In any event, the expanded theory of the taxing power has made the federal government an important factor in the distribution of the national wealth and income.

Our entrance into the war was followed by an expansion and intensification of federal control affecting almost every phase of the national economy. Decisions of the Court involving regulations imposed during World War I had sustained some of the methods of control resorted to during World War II. The first important case dealing with the control of civilians did not involve economic activities.[49] It defined the scope of the war power in such broad terms as would bring within it every "matter and activity so related to war as substantially to affect its conduct and progress." Whatever may have been the reason, the constitutional objections to the economic controls applied during the recent war that the Court had to decide dealt with the express or implied limitations on the war power rather than its scope. The power includes preparation for war as well as waging it. Some of the controls used during the war would be appropriate for peacetime activities connected with preparation for the national defense. The nation could validly continue them during times of peace. The decisions rendered during World War II furnished no test for determining generally how extensively Congress may, while the nation is at peace, regulate the national economy in preparing for its future defense.

49. Hirabayashi v. U.S., (1943) 320 U.S. 81, which sustained a curfew regulation, promulgated in accordance with an Executive Order, which applied to citizens of Japanese ancestry residing in a prescribed area. See also Korematsu v. U.S., (1944) 323 U.S. 214, sustaining an order excluding such citizens from prescribed areas.

The expansion of federal powers has been traced principally through the decisions of the Supreme Court. This is but a part of their total development in recent years. It is the significant part for our purpose because it reveals the processes by which the Constitution has been adapted to changes in political, social, and economic philosophies, and to the progressive integration of the national economy. The Court had a certain body of principles with which to work. It could use, modify, or discard any or all of them, or choose from among them those it deemed best fitted for what it conceived to be its task. In fact, it employed all these methods. The commerce power was expanded by redefining the major concepts developed in prior decisions to determine its scope, and by rejecting theories that had limited its extent by reference to the reserved powers of the states. The first of these methods involved the use of an established and respected principle. The difference between the results formerly obtained by its application and those more recently secured can be explained by the greater judicial recognition since 1933 that the organic nature of our national economy demands that its control be vested in a government capable of acting throughout the whole nation. The result has been that the federal government can define national policies and use its commerce power to make them effective. The taxing power has also been expanded by freeing it of the limits imposed on it by the *Child Labor Tax Case*, and by giving it the status of an independent power. Congress now is able to use it more effectively than before as a regulatory device. Even more important, it has become a potent instrument for effecting any number of social reforms that involve the redistribution of national wealth and income. The Supreme Court has in this field, if not in all others, given more than lip service to the presumption of constitutionality. That is but another way of stating that it accords more weight than has sometimes been the case to the judgment of Congress that the end is legitimate and the means appropriate to its realization. The consequent shift in power from the states to the federal government has impressed many as almost revolutionary. Its full implications cannot now be foreseen, but no one denies that these include a degree of centralized control of the national economy beyond anything thus far attempted during peace time. Nor would anyone deny that it has endowed the nation with a powerful lever for effectuating its views of social reform.[50]

50. For general discussion of the major issues dealt with in this Chapter, see E. S. Corwin, The Twilight of The Supreme Court, (1935); E. S. Corwin, The Commerce Power Versus State Rights, (1936); R. E. Cushman, "Social and Economic Control through Federal Taxation," 18 Minn. Law Rev. 759, (1934); Robert L. Stern, "The Commerce Clause and the National Economy, 1933-1946," 59 Harv. Law Rev. 645, 883 (1946).

III

The Expansion of State Powers Since 1933

IT MAY appear paradoxical to speak of an expansion of state powers after all that has been said about the growth of federal powers. The paradox disappears when account is taken of all the constitutional factors that define those powers. They are residuary powers in the sense that their scope is a function of the content of those delegated to the federal government. Hence every expansion of the latter reduces the potential field of operation of the former. However, there are certain federal powers whose mere existence, even when they remain unused, imposes limits on the states. The commerce power is by far the most important of these. The extent of this limitation has always been treated as a matter for judicial determination. Recent suggestions by some members of the Court that it should intervene only to protect interstate commerce from hostile and discriminatory state action have made little headway and gained practically no acceptance.[1] The Constitu-

1. See dissenting opinion of Justice Black in McCaroll v. Dixie Greyhound Line, (1940) 309 U.S. 176, and of Justice Douglas in So. Pac. Co. v. Arizona, (1945) 325 U.S. 761. See also concurring opinion of the former in Morgan v. Virginia, (1946) 328 U.S. 373, in which he restates his position, concedes that the Court has overruled him on that point, and accepts the

tion subjects the exercise of state powers to other limitations also. Judged by the frequency with which it is invoked, the due process clause of the Fourteenth Amendment is by far the most important of these. Of lesser importance are the equal protection clause of the same Amendment and the contract clause of Section 10 of Article I of the Constitution as originally adopted. The vagueness of the language of these limitations permits the courts to exercise almost unlimited discretion in their application. This is equally true of the implied limitation that neither the federal government nor the states shall so exercise their powers as unduly to hamper the functioning of the other. Some expansion of state powers may occur through judicial relaxation of these various limitations thereon even while the range of permissible federal action is also expanding. The expansion of state powers in most cases has not been at the expense of federal functions at all. The interests once held protected by these limitations have generally been the victims of judicial modifications of their scope.

It has already been shown that the commerce clause has been the most important instrument in the expansion of federal powers, and that this has subjected to federal control many local matters because of their relation to interstate commerce. Some of them were being regulated by the states when Congress intervened, and state control of some came subsequent thereto. In either case, the question arose how far state regulations could still be enforced in the face of federal assumption of some control of the same field. It was a variant of

---

"undue burden upon commerce formula" as the basis for his concurrence with the majority.

the problem that dated back as far as *Cooley v. Board of Port Wardens*.[2] It differed from the earlier one in that the local matter regulated was not itself a part of interstate commerce. That case had divided the subject matter of the commerce power into matters requiring uniformity of treatment on a national basis and those permitting diversity of treatment. It had affirmed the inability of the states to regulate the former, and their competence to regulate the latter in the absence of federal action undertaking to do so. That the only federal legislation concerning pilots had accepted the rules established by the states was held to show a Congressional intent to leave their regulation to the states. The principal opinion in the case expressly excluded from what was being decided the "question how far any regulation of a subject by Congress, may be deemed to operate as an exclusion of all legislation by the States upon the same subject." It was recognized that any state rules that conflicted with a valid federal regulation would be invalid or, as would be said today, unenforceable. That the state pilotage laws did not interfere with any system of regulation established by Congress was among the reasons for sustaining them. The problem of how far the enactment of any legislation by Congress operated to exclude state action, even when not in conflict with federal regulations, was thus posed at a relatively early date with respect to state regulation of interstate transactions. The same question as to the effect of such federal legislation upon state regulation of matters not constituting a part of interstate commerce arose later. The importance of this latter question has

2. (1851) 12 How. 299. See discussion of this case in Chapter I.

transcended that of the former as Congress has used its commerce power more and more to control local matters substantially affecting interstate commerce.

There is no way of preventing federal intervention to regulate local matters under the commerce clause from limiting the potential sphere of state action. The most that the states can hope for is that the Court will so construe federal legislation as to preserve as much of their power as possible. The Court is impotent to help where the state regulations are clearly in conflict with those enacted by Congress. If the conflict is not so clear, it has considerable freedom in choosing between protecting the states' powers and expanding the area of effective federal control. Its discretion becomes the decisive factor when there is no direct conflict. However, the mere absence thereof does not mean that the states' regulations may be enforced. Their enforcement may be incompatible with the execution of the policy of the federal legislation. The decision on such an issue depends largely on how the Court exercises the discretion necessarily vested in it. This is especially true when the question is to what extent federal regulation of some parts of the field indicates a Congressional intent to leave all other parts thereof free from regulation by the states as well as by itself. It is apparent from this analysis that the actual extent to which federal regulation of local matters related to interstate commerce reduces the field for potential state action depends on how the Court uses the discretion belonging to it in deciding issues of the kind just described. The question is, how has it exercised this discretion while the recent broad expansion of federal powers was occurring? In several cases a conflict was discovered by reasoning somewhat forced.[3] In others the finding was clearly justified.[4] The data are insufficient to warrant a conclusion that the Court is tending more and more to use its discretion in favor of restricting state powers whenever possible. But certainly the decisions do not reveal any trend in the opposite direction. The states would not be justified in relying upon the Court to preserve for them the control of local matters by limiting the effect thereon of federal assumption of some control in that field. This is likely to be the case especially with respect to state labor legislation.

The most that could be achieved by use of the technique just described would be to decrease the rate at which federal intervention ousted state control of local matters. It could operate only in that negative manner. The situation is different when the only obstacle to state regulation is the commerce clause itself. A great deal of state legislation has been held invalid because it directly burdened interstate commerce. Much of it that affected such commerce has been sustained because the burden imposed by it was merely indirect. The formulation of the tests in terms of direct and indirect burdens continued in use after 1933 and is used occasionally even today.[5] But there now is a distinct trend in favor of sub-

3. Hines v. Davidowitz, (1941) 312 U.S. 52; Cloverleaf Butter Co. v. Patterson, (1942) 315 U.S. 148; Hill v. Florida ex rel. Watson, (1945) 325 U.S. 538.

4. Illinois Natural Gas Co. v. Central Illinois Public Service Co., (1942) 314 U.S. 498.

5. See, for example, Freeman v. Hewit, (1946) 329 U.S. 249; and Joseph v. Carter & Weekes Stevedoring Co., (1947) 330 U.S. 422, 67 S. Ct. 817. The revival of this approach was vigorously criticized in the concurring opinion of Justice Rutledge in the case first cited above. On the general principles

stituting for them the substantial or insubstantial character of the burden. This has been noticeable especially in the decisions of the last decade. In *Parker v. Brown*[6] the Court sustained a state act applying to the marketing of locally produced fruits a system of control along the lines of the federal statutes regulating the marketing of agricultural products. The bulk of the fruit was destined for the national market after being processed locally. The first argument to sustain it was based on the factor that the transactions regulated were not part of interstate commerce. The opinion next denies that courts are "confined to so mechanical a test." It cites many cases in which broader considerations were relied upon, and expressly states that the local regulations involved were sustained "not because they are 'indirect' rather than 'direct' " but because they were appropriate means for protecting local interests which might never be adequately dealt with by Congress. The "direct-indirect" test has seldom been resorted to by the Court since that decision.[7]

The substitution of one method of formulating a problem for another generally does not change its character. The new method will sometimes be better adapted than the old to directing attention to the fundamental factors that should influence, and in some instances, determine the solution. One aim of the commerce clause

judicially developed in dealing with this problem, see H. W. Bikle, "The Silence of Congress," 41 Harv. Law Rev. 200 (1927); J. B. Sholley, "The Negative Implications of the Commerce Clause," 3 U. of Chicago Law Rev. 556 (1936); N. T. Dowling, "Interstate Commerce and State Power," 27 Va. Law Rev. 1 (1940).

6. (1943) 317 U.S. 341.

7. But see the cases cited in note 5, *supra*.

was the protection of interstate trade against state interference. As a limit on state powers, it is a free trade charter for national commerce. The motives that lead to protective tariffs at the international level are present in each state and have induced a variety of measures to protect the local market from out-of-state competitors. But free trade implies freedom of exportation as well as freedom of importation. The extent to which a state regulation in fact hampers the flow of goods in interstate commerce does not depend upon the nearness of its point of incidence to the transactions that constitute interstate commerce. It depends on the actual results of the regulation. The "direct-indirect" test has fallen into disfavor because it tended to focus attention upon the point of incidence of the regulation upon interstate commerce. The "substantial-insubstantial" test is better devised to suggest an inquiry into the actual results of the regulation upon such commerce. The character and extent of those results is a question of fact. Courts, including the Supreme Court, cannot decide a case involving the validity of a state regulation without answering it, either explicitly or implicitly. That arriving at an answer is not always easy and simple is apparent from *Southern Pacific Company v. Arizona*[8] in which there was a marked difference of opinion on that matter between the Court's majority and minority. Furthermore, judicial excursions into this field of fact-finding in practice may result in Courts substituting their view of the facts for those of the legislature, and in lessening whatever vague influence the presumption of constitutionality may heretofore have had in this field.

8. (1945) 325 U.S. 761.

The minority in the case just referred to made much of these points. But apart from these considerations, determining the existence or nonexistence of the factual burden is but the first step in the judicial process of deciding the validity *vel non* of such state regulations. A burden may exist, and also be a heavy one, and yet the regulation be held valid. The Court must answer the further question "whether the relative weights of the state and national interests involved are such as to make inapplicable the rule, generally observed, that the free flow of interstate commerce and its freedom from local restraints in matters requiring uniformity of regulation are interests safeguarded by the commerce clause from state interference."[9] This involves a balancing of the two interests mentioned in the quotation. The question is posed how far the policy of freedom of trade among the states may be sacrificed to promote a state policy. This is no mere question of fact, but a most difficult problem in value theory. It is fundamentally the same as that which ultimately emerged when the main issue was phrased in terms of the "direct-indirect" test. It is with respect to this element that the problem has remained the same despite the change in the terms of its formulation. But this is precisely its most decisive element.

The Court's approach to problems of this nature in many cases prior to 1933 did not differ greatly from that now favored. It was aware then as now that the state regulation under attack had to have some effects upon interstate commerce, and many of its opinions of that time are at pains to indicate their character and extent

9. At pp. 770 and 771 of 325 U.S.

in language no vaguer than that found in some recent decisions. Nor was it unaware of the fact that it had to weigh the competing claims of state policies and the freedom of interstate commerce from state interferences in determining whether the burden thereon was "direct" or "indirect." The current approach could be used to expand state powers if (a) the "substantial-insubstantial" tests made it more difficult to discover that the effects of the state regulation burdened interstate commerce, or (b) if the Court were more inclined than formerly to permit some sacrifice of the interests of that commerce to promote state policies, or (c) if both of these conditions existed. The cases involving exercises of the states' police powers are rather inconclusive. There is no certainty that it will be more difficult to show that the effects of a regulation constitute a substantial burden than it formerly was to prove that they were a direct burden. In two important recent decisions the state act was held invalid after a rather complete factual analysis of the burden imposed on interstate commerce thereby. Both involved regulations applied to interstate transportation.[10] In another involving such transportation the state act was sustained.[11] The record is similarly inconclusive where the matters regulated were not a part of interstate commerce. Resort to the new test is likely to produce a more intelligent consideration of whether the burden exists and what is its extent. But it cannot be said to have increased greatly the likelihood of decisions favor-

10. Southern Pac. v. Arizona, (1945) 325 U.S. 761; Morgan v. Virginia, (1946) 328 U.S. 373.
11. South Carolina State Highway Dept. v. Barnwell Bros., Inc., (1938) 303 U.S. 177.

able to state legislation, although there is some evidence that local policies may receive more favorable recognition in their competition with interstate commerce than heretofore. The virtual overruling of *Di Santo v. Pennsylvania*[12] by *California v. Thompson*, [13] and the practical limiting of *Sioux Remedy Co. v. Cope*[14] by *Union Brokerage Co. v. Jensen*,[15] point in that direction. But the fate meted out to the California statute that made it a misdemeanor to bring into the state persons known to be indigent warns us to proceed cautiously in drawing inferences as to trends on the basis of limited data.[16] California was told in no uncertain terms that the commerce clause prohibits attempts on the part of any single state to "isolate itself from difficulties common to all of them by restraining the transportation of persons and property across its borders." The opinion contains a curious suggestion which implies that the inability of nonresident indigents to secure a change in policy by exerting pressure upon the California legislature was a factor calling forth the condemnation of the commerce clause. Here is a new weapon to use against state regulation of interstate commerce. It has vast possibliities in the hands of a Court that is sensitive to the tides of political opinion. It was asserted that "large-scale interstate migration" produced by the depression was a

12. (1927) 273 U.S. 34.
13. (1941) 313 U.S. 109.
14. (1914) 235 U.S. 197.
15. (1944) 322 U.S. 202.
16. Edwards v. California, (1941) 314 U.S. 160. Three of the Justices held the California statute invalid solely for conflict with the privileges and immunities clause of the 14th Amendment. Justice Jackson, while conceding that it could be so held on the basis of the commerce clause, preferred to rest its invalidity on that same clause of the 14th Amendment.

matter of national concern requiring uniformity of treatment which only the federal government could furnish.[17] The scope of the subject matter requiring such uniformity of rule is as capable of judicial expansion today as when the doctrine was invented. It can be expanded to restrict state powers whenever the majority of the Court disapproves the policy the state is aiming to enforce. For some time to come such disapproval is more likely to be directed at regulations interfering with what are called "human rights" than those intended to control business. So far as the decisions here reviewed involved value judgments, they indicate that the decisive factor is the kind of policy the state is seeking to promote. They do not show any definite trend toward greater tolerance for state policies generally. This may appear when further decisions increase the data from which generalizations can be constructed. The trend towards more and more governmental regulation is likely to continue. Should experience show that effective controls are more likely to be achieved by some degree of decentralization, it is almost certain that more and more local policies involving some burden upon interstate commerce will secure the Court's approval. The tools for that have always been available. Recent decisions have improved them.

The social and economic forces that produced the expansion of federal powers were responsible also for a concurrent growth in state functions. Their performance

17. That the commerce clause would permit Congress to prohibit interstate migrations is implicit in the theories enunicated by it in United States v. Darby, (1941) 312 U.S. 100. It may well be questioned whether such legislation would be sustained as not violative of the due process clause of the 5th Amendment.

increased the cost of state government. The natural result was a search for new sources of revenue or a more intensive cultivation of those already in use. That the commerce clause imposed some restrictions upon a state's taxing power had been established in 1827 by *Brown v. Maryland*.[18] A rather formidable body of constitutional law had developed since that time attempting to define the extent of those restrictions.[19] It was inevitable that taxpayers in a position to do so would invoke the commerce clause to test the validity of any new tax bearing even the remotest relation to interstate or foreign commerce. That existing precedents stood in the way did not deter states from levying taxes formerly condemned. Precedents were being readily distinguished and even overruled. The Court was presented with numerous opportunities to prevent further shrinkage of the states' taxing powers by refusing to extend the limits imposed thereon by the commerce clause. It also had several to expand them by removing limits set by former decisions. In no case has it increased the restrictions beyond those established prior to 1933.

The important decisions since 1933 dealing with the relation of the commerce clause to the states' taxing powers have involved license taxes however measured, and taxes that were in effect measured by gross receipts or gross income whatever the formal subject of the tax. A sales tax on specific transactions is for practical purposes one on gross receipts. The reason why such taxes were so frequently before the Court was that

18. (1827) 12 Wheat. 419.
19. See Rottschaefer, Handbook of American Constitutional Law, Secs. 163–174. See also J. M. Landis, "The Commerce Clause as a Restriction on State Taxation," 20 Mich. Law Rev. 50 (1921).

states were increasingly resorting to general sales taxes to meet revenue needs caused by the depression. It had become a well established principle that the commerce clause prohibited both the state of the buyer and seller from taxing interstate sales or the business of making such sales. Confronted with this, the buyers' states sought means to protect their local producers and merchants. Compensating use taxes were imposed upon the local use or consumption of goods acquired by residents through interstate sales. Other states sought to meet their revenue needs by imposing taxes on gross income or on local privileges measured by gross income. A formidable array of decisions could be cited to prove their invalidity under the commerce clause so far as gross income or receipts from interstate commerce entered into their computation. It would have required extremely heroic efforts to so distinguish or reinterpret them as to remove them as obstacles to new devices for reaching such income or receipts. With respect to none of these taxes was it a foregone conclusion that the commerce clause would invalidate it wholly or even in any of its applications. Many of the decisions relied upon to prove them unconstitutional dated back to a period when the emphasis had been put upon the protection of interstate commerce and the revenue needs of the states slighted. The suggestion that these latter deserved more consideration was implicit in the protest of Justice Stone in his concurring opinion in *Helson v. Kentucky*,[20] decided in 1929, that he could find no "practical justification . . . for an interpretation of the commerce clause which would relieve those engaged in

20. (1929) 279 U.S. 245.

interstate commerce from their fair share of the expense of government of the states in which they operate by exempting them from the payment of a tax of general application, which is neither aimed at nor discriminates against interstate commerce." This proved to be an important factor in defining the course of subsequent developments.

The subject of each of the taxes mentioned in the preceding paragraph differs from that of the others. Their measure is practically the same although gross receipts denote something not quite identical with gross income. The difference may be ignored since it played no part in the Court's reasoning. The cases involving any one of them are cited as authorities in passing on the validity of the others. It will be convenient, however, to consider the use tax cases separately and first. It had been decided prior to 1933 that a use tax, when levied on gasoline used as the motive power for operating an interstate ferry, was invalid as a tax on the privilege of transacting such commerce.[21] The first case to reach the Court after 1933 concerned a tax on materials and equipment brought in from outside the taxing state by a contractor who used them therein on a local construction job.[22] It did not apply to the use of goods on which the state sales tax had been paid, and a credit was allowed for any retail sales tax paid in any other state. It was sustained because it was neither upon the operations of interstate commerce nor so measured or conditioned as to hamper or discriminate against transactions therein. The wholly local character of the event

21. Helson v. Kentucky, (1929) 279 U.S. 245.
22. Henneford v. Silas Mason Co., Inc., (1937) 300 U.S. 577.

on which liability for it accrued was an important formal factor in the decision, and distinguished it from *Helson v. Kentucky*. But more fundamental than this was its purpose and result in equalizing competition between local and out-of-state vendors. A purely mechanical test was used to sustain a California use tax on tangible personalty purchased in another state for immediate or ultimate installation in an interstate railway facility in the taxing state.[23] The Court discovered or invented a "taxable moment" when the goods that were directly installed for use in transportation had ceased to move in interstate commerce but had not yet "begun to be consumed in interstate operation." This certainly limits the *Helson Case* but so far that has never been overruled. However, states had discovered other "taxable moments" at which the equivalent of a use tax could be imposed, and the Court before 1933 had held valid several devices for circumventing its effects.[24] It is worth noting that the California tax statute allowed no credit for any sales tax paid to another state. The principal importance of these "use tax" cases is their recognition of the right of a state to offset the discrimination in favor of interstate sales resulting from the invalidity of sales taxes on interstate sales. The economic interests of the buyer's state was beginning to receive recognition.

Use taxes have never been easy to collect and have

23. Southern Pacific Co. v. Gallagher, (1939) 306 U.S. 167.
24. See, for example, Edelman v. Boeing Air Transport, Inc., (1933) 289 U.S. 249, and Nashville, C. & St. L. Ry. Co. v. Wallace, (1933) 288 U.S. 249, sustaining excise taxes on the storage or withdrawal from storage of gasoline stored or withdrawn to furnish motive power for interstate transportation.

frequently been evaded. States imposing them have sought to prevent this by imposing the duty to collect the tax upon the vendor. Attempts to do so have been challenged for conflict with both the commerce clause and the due process clause of the Fourteenth Amendment. In the first case raising these issues the vendor, a foreign corporation, maintained an office in the taxing state. Its sole business therein consisted of interstate sales to local consumers from whom it was required to collect the state use tax levied on the use of the goods thus sold.[25] In the next case the vendor, again a foreign corporation, had a retail store in Iowa, the taxing state. It also made interstate sales therein through catalogue solicitation involving no activities on the part of its Iowa agents. It objected to the collection of the use tax on the goods thus sold. Imposing that duty was held to constitute neither a regulation of, nor a substantial burden upon, interstate commerce.[26] That the vendor incurred costs, and ran the risk of losses, was deemed of no account. That it would be at a disadvantage with its mail order competitors who had no retail outlets in Iowa was held no objection at all since Iowa could exact from it a price for benefits conferred which its competitors did not share. The most recent case went even further.[27] As in the others, the vendor was a foreign corporation. Its only connection with the taxing state, Iowa, was that its salesmen solicited orders therein which were filled by shipments from outside the state. The statute was sustained as applied to even such a

25. Felt & Tarrant Mfg. Co. v. Gallagher, (1939) 306 U.S. 62.
26. Nelson v. Sears, Roebuck & Co., (1941) 312 U.S. 359.
27. General Trading Co. v. State Tax Comm. of Iowa, (1944) 322 U.S. 335.

case on the authority of the two cases just discussed. The opinion in some of its parts appears to view the tax as one levied upon the vendor, but, despite that, concludes that the duty to collect the tax from the ultimate consumer may be imposed upon it. A dissenting opinion denies that a state can exact such a condition from a person who is beyond its jurisdiction to tax as the price for the privilege of engaging therein in interstate commerce. It is inconceivable that the doctrine of these cases can be extended any further. However small the relief from the limits of the commerce clause attributable to the cases sustaining state use taxes, these decisions definitely expand state powers by refusing to use the commerce and due process clauses to prevent states from devising effective measures for the collection of a valid tax.

The gross income, gross receipts, and sales tax cases are so closely related that they can best be considered together. The gross income and receipts tax cases will be included whether those factors constitute the tax subject or merely a measure of a license or privilege tax. This is in line with what the Court itself has done. The first cases decided after 1933 involved privilege taxes measured by the gross receipts from broadcasting[28] and from loading and discharging cargoes in interstate and foreign commerce.[29] The rule as developed

28. Fisher's Blend Station, Inc. v. State Tax Commission, (1936) 297 U.S. 650.

29. Puget Sound Stevedoring Co. v. Tax Commission of State of Washington, (1937) 302 U.S. 90. The principle of this case was recently followed in Joseph v. Carter & Weekes Stevedoring Co., (1947) 330 U.S. 422, 67 S. Ct. 815. There was no dissent in the former of these cases, but four Justices dissented in the latter so far as the tax was held prohibited by the commerce clause.

prior to 1933 that taxes on, or measured by, the gross receipts from such commerce violated the commerce clause was rigorously applied and both taxes were held invalid. The first important inroad upon that doctrine was made in *Western Live Stock v. Bureau of Revenue*,[30] decided in the same term of Court as the last case referred to. The tax was imposed on the gross advertising revenues of a trade journal with a circulation in several states. The advertisers included both local and out-of-state firms whose advertising had been solicited through the channels of interstate commerce. The commerce clause was held not to invalidate the tax. The case was readily distinguishable from the two mentioned above in that the activity whose gross earnings were taxed could in no sense be said to constitute interstate commerce. What lends importance to the case is not its decision but its new approach to the problem of taxing the gross earnings from interstate commerce. The essence of that problem is the reconciliation of the right of the states that interstate commerce pay its way with the freedom of such commerce from cumulative exactions not laid on local business. Judged by the standards implicit in this approach, taxes on, or measured by, the gross receipts from interstate commerce would be invalid only if they imposed upon commerce "burdens of such a nature as to be capable, in point of substance, of being imposed . . . with equal right by every state which the commerce touches, merely because interstate commerce is being done, so that without the protection of the commerce clause it would bear cumulative burdens not imposed on local

30. (1938) 303 U.S. 250.

commerce."[31] It was such trade barriers which the commerce clause was intended to remove. The new principle is asserted to give consistency to the body of prior decisions. The tax in question was imposed upon a taxable subject and was reasonable in amount. Its only burden on interstate commerce was that it represented an added cost. So far as it reflected a value attributable to the taxpayer's interstate business, the burden thereon was too remote to condemn it. Furthermore, since all the acts conditioning its accrual and amount were local, no other state could duplicate it and thus expose interstate commerce to cumulative burdens. Such was the reasoning by which its validity was upheld. The method followed furnished the pattern for all subsequent decisions involving similar taxes, and even such unrelated taxes as those on property used in interstate commerce.

The application of these principles runs into difficulties where the activities whose gross income is taxed are conducted in more than one state. That was the situation in *Gwin, White & Prince, Inc. v. Henneford.*[32] The taxpayer's business consisted in acting as brokers for fruit growers' cooperatives in several states in marketing the members' product in the national market. Its activities were thus in aid of interstate commerce, and were carried on in several states. The tax was on

31. It is arguable that this principle had been implicitly recognized in prior cases involving state taxes on, or measured by, the gross earnings from interstate commerce. However, in no prior case had it received the explicit recognition and formulation given it by this case. See T. R. Powell, "New Light on Gross Receipts Taxes," 53 Harv. Law Rev. 909 (1940); W. B. Lockhart, "State Tax Barriers to Interstate Trade," 53 Harv. Law Rev. 1253 (1940); W. B. Lockhart, "Gross Receipts Taxes on Interstate Transportation and Communication," 57 Harv. Law Rev. 40 (1943).

32. (1939) 305 U.S. 434.

the privilege of conducting that business and was measured by the compensation it received for its services. The case involved only the compensation received for services rendered for producers in the taxing state. The tax was not apportioned to reflect the fact that extra-state interstate commerce activities had produced part of the gross receipts by which it was measured. It was this factor that rendered it invalid. The principle that would sustain it would also permit the other states in which any part of those activities were conducted to tax the tax payer's entire gross receipts therefrom. This would subject interstate commerce to the risk of multiple burdens merely because the transactions involved constituted such commerce. It is immaterial that the other states have not imposed a similar tax. Since local commerce was not subject to that danger, the practical operation of a tax based on total gross earnings would discriminate against interstate commerce. Justice Black alone dissented. He repeated his views that Congress, and not the Court, was authorized to protect interstate commerce from this class of risk. He feared that the principle applied by the majority would afford "big corporations" an opportunity to evade taxes which small local businesses would be unable to escape. The same principles had been used to limit the effective range of operation of the Indiana gross income tax law.[33]

The Indiana gross income tax is, in practical operation, a sales tax imposed by the seller's state so far as such income is derived from sales. If the sale is an interstate sale the tax is in effect a sales tax on interstate sales. The principle that the commerce clause pro-

33. J. D. Adams Mfg. Co. v. Storen, (1938) 304 U.S. 307.

hibited their taxation by the states had been firmly established well before 1933.[34] A subsequent local sale, even in the original package, could be taxed. That was the state of the law when the Court reviewed the problem anew in *McGoldrick v. Berwind-White Coal Mining Company*.[35] This involved a municipal sales tax imposed under the following circumstances. The vendor, a foreign corporation with respect to the state under whose authority the tax was imposed, maintained a local sales office in New York, the city levying the tax. The contracts for the sales in issue were made there through the local sales office. They contemplated an interstate transportation of the coal which was their subject matter, and called for its delivery within the limits of New York City. This was an interstate sale if ever there was one. Its taxation was upheld by a divided Court. A state tax was said to be invalid under the commerce clause only if its imposition operated as a regulation of interstate commerce to such an extent as impaired the power of Congress to regulate that commerce. Nothing is gained by reformulating the constitutional problem in these terms. However, the majority opinion soon returns to fundamentals, rephrasing the problem before it in the language used in the *Western Live Stock Case*. No small part of the opinion is concerned with a rather confused and unsuccessful attempt to reinterpret a long line of prior decisions so as to transform them into decisions sustaining this sales tax. Those decisions are subjected

34. See Rottschaefer, Handbook on American Constitutional Law, Secs. 170, 171.

35. (1940) 309 U.S. 33. See W. B. Lockhart, "The Sales Tax in Interstate Commerce," 52 Harv. Law Rev. 617 (1939); S. Morrison, "State Taxation of Interstate Commerce," 36 Ill. Law Rev. 727 (1924).

to rather violent treatment. Some importance was attached to the fact that the delivery, described as the taxable event, occurred within the city. This appears to have been a factor supporting the contention that a tax, levied as was this one, could not be duplicated by any other state. The minority rightly objected that the local incident thus availed of was as much a part of interstate commerce as the interstate transportation of the coal, and that, even if the tax could be sustained on that basis, it would not justify a tax on the whole transaction by taxing its total gross receipts. It also called inadequate the majority's argument based on the use tax cases. But its most effective blow was that in which it demonstrated the multiple burdens that could be imposed on interstate commerce under the theory of the prevailing opinion if each state exercised its taxing power within the limits permitted thereby.

The limits of the principle adopted in the *Berwind-White Coal Company Case* have not yet been definitely determined. Four years after its decision the Court considered another sales tax imposed on an interstate sale by the buyer's state. The facts in *McLeod v. J. E. Dilworth Company*[36] differed from those in the earlier case. The differences appear to have been material. The vendor maintained no office in Arkansas, the taxing state. The sales were solicited by drummers or through the mail, and all orders had to be accepted in Tennessee where the vendor had its place of business. Title to the goods was assumed to pass on delivery to the carrier in Tennessee. The tax was held invalid because the sales were consummated there. This factor had been declared

36. (1944) 322 U.S. 327.

to be irrelevant in the *Berwind-White Coal Company Case*. That case was distinguished on the grounds that the vendor therein maintained a sales office in New York City, that the sales contracts were made there, and that the vendor completed its sales there by making delivery there. If these distinctions are valid, the scope of the *Berwind-White Coal Company Case* would be severely limited. No later decision has fully resolved this issue. No subsequent statement by the Court can be pointed to that furnishes clear guidance to the answer. However, the *Dilworth Company Case* is also significant for its rejection of the theory, implicit in the reasoning of the *Berwind-White Coal Company Case*, that a state's power to impose a sales tax on interstate sales is defined by its power to subject the goods thus introduced into it to a local use tax. This rejection was vigorously opposed in the dissenting opinion on the score that the economic effects of such a use tax are indistinguishable from those of a comparable sales tax on the interstate sale. It is these economic effects that measure the degree of inequality imposed on local trade when interstate sales are relieved of a sales tax. The minority would treat as the decisive factor the occurrence of a taxable event in the buyer's state which imposes the tax, and hold solicitation and delivery therein sufficient support for such a tax. It rightly considers the decision a retreat from the *Berwind-White Coal Company Case*.

The power of the seller's state to impose a sales tax, or its equivalent, has been considered by the Court in a series of cases involving the Indiana Gross Income Tax. The first of them was decided in 1938; the most recent one late in 1946. The former has already been noted and requires no further consideration. Those decided thereafter but before the most recent decision added nothing to an understanding or solution of the problems involved. The recent case, *Freeman v. Hewit*,[37] is extremely important. It involved a tax on the net proceeds of a sale of securities on the New York Stock Exchange effected by a resident of Indiana through a local broker. The tax was held violative of the commerce clause. The cases thus far discussed had practically avoided using any reasoning that conditioned the validity of a state tax upon its direct or indirect incidence upon interstate commerce. They had made this to depend upon whether it discriminated against such commerce or was of such character as would permit its duplication by other states. The majority in the instant case reverts to a test that many had assumed to have been discarded. That a tax is laid upon "the very process of interstate commerce" necessarily impedes it and thus frustrates the purpose of the commerce clause to prevent states "from exacting toll from those engaged in national commerce." Justice Rutledge, in his concurring opinion, objects vigorously to the reversion to this test.

The majority does not reject the view that interstate commerce should pay its just share of state expenses. But it gives the idea a quite novel and startling turn. There had been no previous explicit attempts to either define what would constitute its fair share or indicate by what tax device this result was to be secured. The aim of permitting the buyer's state to tax the interstate sale is to deprive it of a competitive advantage over the local sale. It seems to have been assumed that

37. (1946) 329 U.S. 249.

the just share was a similar tax no higher than that imposed on the local sale. This has its roots in the belief that it was a reasonable method for protecting a legitimate interest of the buyer's state. The matter is not so simple when the tax is imposed by the seller's state. The tax is scarcely a device for protecting its own producers against out-of-state competition, and is a positive hindrance to access to the interstate market. It could be availed of to conserve its resources for the state's own people, but this would be at the expense of interstate commerce. It could also be used by a state possessing a monopoly of some resource to shift to consumers in other states a part of its own governmental costs. That too would likely be at the expense of interstate commerce. It is difficult to find here any policy that would be held to justify the restraint that the tax would impose on interstate commerce unless the mere raising of revenue for state purposes be such. But that suggests no immediate test of what would be the just share that the interstate sale might be called upon to bear nor what method of taxation should be used to realize that end. The majority rejects the view that the mere levy of a sales tax on local sales justifies a like tax on interstate sales. This must imply that the just share of interstate commerce need not necessarily be met by a tax similar and equal to that imposed on local commerce. While it furnishes no index to what would be that just share, it makes it easier to understand the majority's interpretation of the principle that interstate commerce must pay its way. The Court in effect reserves the right to control the method by which a state may apply it. It may not do so by a "direct imposition on that very freedom of commercial flow" which has always been "the ward of the Commerce Clause." The seller's state at least is precluded thereby from making that commerce pay its way by a tax on its gross receipts. Various alternative taxes are suggested for making interstate commerce pay its way, such as property taxes, manufacturing taxes, or excise taxes for the privilege of engaging in local business. The suggestions have merely complicated the problem of determining interstate commerce's fair tax contribution to state expenses. They have made its solution by the courts next to impossible. Though the language of the opinion is general, it was undoubtedly intended to apply only to the seller's state since the instant case shows no intention of modifying the *Berwind-White Coal Company Case.*

The concurring opinion of Justice Rutledge deserves consideration. It was induced by his fears that the majority left in doubt whether it intended to qualify or repudiate *Adams Manufacturing Company v. Storen.*[38] That was the first important case involving the Indiana Gross Income Tax as applied to interstate commerce. The Court had found the vice therein as thus applied in that it included in its measure "without apportionment," the gross receipts from interstate commerce. The failure to base the decision in *Freeman v. Hewit* on that principle was responsible for Justice Rutledge's fears. The importance of his opinion lies in its thorough examination of the current status of the law with respect to the validity of gross earnings and sales taxes under the commerce clause. He strongly

38. (1938) 304 U.S. 307.

objects to the reversion to the "direct incidence" test as a return to the "formalism of another day." He shows its inadequacy as an explanation of the actual decisions, and does everything possible to preserve in full force the principles developed in the *Western Live Stock Case* and the subsequent cases that adopted and applied them. This is but a preliminary to a new analysis of the entire problem raised by these taxes. Three alternatives are presented for reconciling the interests of the states with those of interstate commerce. The first is to stop them at the source by prohibiting them unless apportioned. The second is to permit either the buyer's or seller's state, but not both, to impose such taxes. The last is to determine in each case whether the state that has imposed it can do so without in fact incurring the danger that another will impose a like tax. His own choice, asserted to be the most consistent with the purposes of the commerce clause, is to permit both states to tax. The buyer's state would be allowed to tax the entire proceeds from interstate commerce without apportionment if only the tax be kept nondiscriminatory. The seller's state's power would be a qualified one. It would be required to allow as a credit against its tax the full amount of any tax paid or due to the buyer's state. This presumably means paid or due with respect to the same interstate transaction. The practical application of this principle would not be so difficult if each state levied a specific single rate sales tax thereon. It would involve great difficulty if each taxed the gross receipts from the same transaction through their inclusion in an aggregate subjected to a graduated tax. How would the credit be computed in such case? Justice

Rutledge had put forth the same theory in his opinion in the *Dilworth Company Case*. In neither does he claim it to represent the actual law. He seems convinced that the combined effect of the *Berwind-White Coal Company Case* and the instant case is to give the buyer's state full power to tax without apportionment while denying the seller's state the right to tax interstate transactions and their gross receipts by even an apportioned tax. That position is probably correct.

The fact that the New York City sales tax involved in the *Berwind-White Coal Company Case* was conditioned upon a local activity, viz., the delivery of the goods in the city, was at least a factor in sustaining it. The Court has twice distinguished it from other cases on that score. Chief Justice Hughes had criticized the majority for supporting the tax on that basis. He viewed the local delivery as an integral part of interstate commerce as much so as was interstate transportation. The case of *Nippert v. Richmond*,[39] decided in 1946, gave the Court an opportunity to test the implications of its own reasoning. The city of Richmond required all solicitors to pay an annual fixed-sum license fee plus a tax on their gross earnings for the preceding year. The case involved only the validity of the former when applied to a solicitor for out-of-state firms. The exaction was indistinguishable from those held invalid in the "drummer cases." The city contended that their authority had been impaired by the recent decisions, especially that in the *Berwind-White Case*. It justified its own tax as one levied on a local event, i.e., solicitation, resting its claim squarely on that case. The Court avoided

39. (1946) 327 U.S. 416.

this logical implication of its own position by invoking the other considerations and broader policy on which it had rested its earlier decision. It was thus forced to re-examine its theory. The validity of a tax on a local incident of interstate commerce was said to depend upon its actual or potential effects thereon. If it operated to suppress or unduly burden it, or discriminated against it by subjecting it to a burden not placed upon competing local business, then it would be invalid and the mere fact that it was conditioned upon a local incident would not save it. The tax was found unduly burdensome largely on the basis of factors that distinguished it from the New York City sales tax. The distinctions relied upon to establish its greater exclusionary effects included (1) that it was for a fixed amount that bore no inherent relation to the volume of business or the returns therefrom; (2) that its economic incidence was on the initial step of the interstate transaction rather than on the completed transaction; and (3) that the cumulative burden upon interstate commerce might easily become prohibitive if other cities should adopt the device. While not on its face discriminatory since it applied also to solicitors for local firms, the Court found that in practice it would discriminate against interstate commerce. Both lines of reasoning contributed to holding it invalid. Some of the considerations advanced by the Court would not apply to that part of the tax based on the solicitor's earnings. That part would be valid if the principles of the *Western Live Stock Case* may be extended to such earnings, or if the *Berwind-White Case* is to be given its full effect. However, *Puget Sound Stevedoring Company v. Tax Com-*

mission[40] militates against this conclusion, and it has never yet been overruled. The dissent in *Freeman v. Hewit*, the Indiana gross income case last considered, sought to sustain the tax therein involved as one levied on a local activity, the management of the investment portfolio of the Indiana vendor of securities on the New York Stock Exchange. The question arises whether the theory of *Nippert v. Richmond* extends to local activities that are not an integral part of interstate commerce. The decision itself does not require its extension thereto. Nor does any of its reasoning. It is unlikely to be so extended except where the tax clearly discriminates against interstate commerce. No new principle is needed for that. It may be safely assumed that the Court did not intend this case to impair the force of those decisions that sustain state taxes on a local subject that is not an integral part of interstate commerce. An excise on manufacturing for distribution in the national market may be taken as an illustration of such a tax.[41]

The only case involving other forms of state taxes that merits at least passing notice is the *Northwest Airlines, Inc. Case.*[42] Minnesota, the state of domicile, imposed its property tax upon its entire fleet of planes, all of which were continuously employed in interstate transportation on regular routes with scheduled stopping places in Minnesota and five other states. All were present in Minnesota from time to time while in transit in the course of those flights, and also for periodic overhauling and repair. On Minnesota's tax day only some

40. (1937) 302 U.S. 90. See also note 29, *supra.*
41. See American Mfg. Co. v. St. Louis, (1919) 250 U.S. 459.
42. N.W. Airlines, Inc. v. Minnesota, (1944) 322 U.S. 292.

of them were present. Airlines contended that the commerce clause and due process clause of the Fourteenth Amendment prohibited Minnesota from taxing planes not present within it on that day. It did so on the assumption that those constitutional provisions required the domiciliary state to adjust its taxing power to the liability of at least some part of its fleet of planes to taxation by other states. No prior case had ever so held, and the issue had not been raised in the *Miller Case*,[43] which presented a similar situation with respect to the rolling stock of an interstate railroad. Here was an opportunity to extend to the property used in interstate commerce the same protection against multiple state taxation that the commerce clause had been held to confer upon interstate sales. The dissenting opinion of Chief Justice Stone is a forceful argument for Airlines' claim that the method of apportionment applied to railroad rolling stock should be required in order to protect interstate commerce from the burden of multiple state taxation of its planes. He denied that domicile was a relevant factor so far as the commerce clause affected the validity of the tax. The majority, however, gave decisive weight to domicile in sustaining the tax against objections based on both the commerce and due process clauses. It evinced a fidelity to an old precedent that was unusual for the Court as then composed, and one in which the precise issue had not even been considered. It passed on to Congress the task of protecting commerce against the domiciliary state's taxing power because it did not wish "to indulge in constitutional

43. New York ex rel. N.Y. Cent. & H.R.R. Co. v. Miller, (1906) 202 U.S. 584.

innovation." While this decision may not have expanded state taxing powers, it did protect them against diminution at a time when principles developed by the Court could readily have been applied to do so.

The taxing power of the states has benefited more than their police power from the Court's decisions concerning the extent to which the commerce clause itself limits their powers. However difficult it may be to determine the precise extent of their expansion, it is still true that they may impose some taxes that the commerce clause as construed prior to 1933 prevented them from levying. The reversion to the older and more formal "direct burden" test that occurred in *Freeman v. Hewit* may retard the rate of any further expansion. It is unlikely to result in a movement that will whittle down that already achieved. The most important single factor responsible for freeing this power from some of the limits imposed upon it by earlier decisions was the judicial acceptance of the view that interstate commerce should pay its way, and its use as a factor in determining whether a given state tax unduly burdened that commerce. A tender regard for some precedents may occasionally deter the Court from giving sanction to all of its implications but it is here to stay. Much remains to be done to give it a clearer and more definite meaning. The second factor that has influenced recent developments has been the judicial desire to reduce the area within which an immunity from taxation based on the commerce clause gives interstate commerce a competitive advantage over local commerce. There is little likelihood that this will lose its force. While this expansion has been proceeding, there

have been no decisions construing the commerce clause
that deprived the states of power to tax anything which
they could tax prior to 1933.

The expansion of state powers thus far considered was
secured wholly through judicial action. A technique for
freeing the states of some of the limits imposed upon
their powers by the commerce clause had already been
developed prior to 1933. The states had found that
clause a serious handicap to their enforcement of the
policy embodied in their legislation prohibiting the
manufacture and sale of intoxicating liquors. It had
been construed to prevent its application to original
package sales within them, at least without the assent
of Congress. The advocates of prohibition seized upon
that qualification and procured federal legislation
subjecting intoxicants to their laws upon their arrival
within them. This was held a valid regulation under
the commerce power which gave the states no power
not already possessed but merely removed an impediment to the enforcement of state laws "created by the
absence of a specific utterance" on the part of Congress.[44] Subsequent federal legislation extended the
protection of this state policy by prohibiting the interstate transportation of intoxicants into any state for
use therein in violation of its laws. This also was held
a valid exercise of the commerce power in *Clark Distilling Company v. Western Maryland Railroad Company*.[45] The reasoning of the Court starts from the
premise that Congress could have absolutely prohibited
the shipment of intoxicants in interstate commerce.

44. See Chapter I, *supra*.
45. (1917) 242 U.S. 311.

Since the statute falls short of an exercise of Congress' complete power over intoxicants, to deny its validity would be to invalidate a regulation of commerce because it did not exhaust Congress' full power over the subject. This impressed the Court as the manifest absurdity which it was. An important part of the opinion is devoted to meeting the contention that the decision laid the basis for subjecting interstate commerce in all articles to state control. This fear was said to be unwarranted because "the exceptional nature of the subject here regulated is the basis upon which the exceptional power exerted must rest and affords no ground for any fear that such power may be constitutionally extended to things which it may not, consistently with the guarantees of the Constitution, embrace." Its exceptional nature consisted in its liability to a degree of governmental regulation that would have violated "constitutional guarantees" if generally applied to other subjects than intoxicants. The "constitutional guarantees" are not designated but the context shows the reference to be to the due process and similar constitutional provisions. The net result was that Congress might exercise its commerce power to aid a state regulatory policy if (1) the subject of the regulation was such that Congress could close the channels of interstate commerce to it, and (2) if it was such that the state regulation applied to it did not conflict with the federal constitutional guaranties of due process and similar provisions.

The principle of federal cooperation in aid of the enforcement of state policies through Congress' exercise of the commerce power was thus rather narrowly limited prior to 1933. It has since been considerably extended. The first expansion occurred when Congress applied to prison-made goods the technique that had received judicial sanction with respect to intoxicants. A statute along the lines of that sustained in *In re Rahrer*[46] was held valid in *Whitfield v. Ohio.*[47] One adopting the method of that sustained in the *Clark Distilling Company Case* was upheld in *Kentucky Whip & Collar Company v. Illinois Central Railroad Company.*[48] Both were decided before *Hammer v. Dagenhart* had been overruled. The *Whitfield Case* was decided wholly on the authority of *In re Rahrer*. The opinion therein does not even cite the *Clark Distilling Company Case*. It expressly declines to decide whether there are any limits on Congress' power to remove "the impediment to state control presented by the unbroken-package doctrine." It is a forthright holding that Congress may do so to aid a state to protect its free labor from the evil of competition with goods produced by "the enforced and unpaid or underpaid convict labor of the prison." That this is an evil is reinforced by citing federal legislation prohibiting the importation of such goods from abroad. The ultimate basis of the decision in the *Kentucky Whip & Collar Company Case* is also the legitimacy of the state policy which Congress sought to protect. The federal statute itself is viewed as a proper recognition of the interests of free labor. There are grounds for holding that the state's regulatory policy must relate to a subject matter that the due process and similar

46. (1891) 140 U.S. 545.
47. (1936) 297 U.S. 431.
48. (1937) 299 U.S. 334.

constitutional provisions do not prevent it from regulating in its internal commerce. As stated in the opinion:

"The pertinent point is that where the subject of commerce is one as to which the power of the State may constitutionally be exerted by restriction or prohibition in order to prevent harmful consequences, the Congress may, if it sees fit, put forth its power to regulate interstate commerce so as to prevent that commerce from being used to impede the carrying out of the state policy."[49]

The Court could not, in this case, avoid considering the view expressed in the *Clark Distilling Company Case* that the principle was limited by the "exceptional nature of the subject" there involved. It rejected the view that the statute was invalid "merely because the horse collars and harness" were useful and harmless articles. It did so on the basis of decisions sustaining the power of Congress to prohibit the interstate transportation of stolen automobiles. It is a fair conclusion from these decisions that Congress may use its power to prohibit interstate commerce in aid of any state regulatory policy that does not discriminate against interstate commerce nor violate such federal constitutional guaranties as the due process and equal protection clauses of the Fourteenth Amendment. Its subject matter is no longer a factor. As the *Darby Case* has freed Congress' power to prohibit interstate commerce from any limits based on the commerce clause, the assumption made in the *Clark Distilling Company Case* is no longer of any importance. It may be remarked that it is not quite clear why conformity of the state regulatory policy with the constitutional guarantees mentioned

49. At p. 351 of 299 U.S.

should define the limit of Congress' power in this matter.

The decision in 1944 in the *South-Eastern Underwriters Association Case*[50] had held insurance conducted across state lines to constitute interstate commerce. It immediately created doubts as to the validity of existing state laws regulating and taxing that business. They were soon resolved, so far as Congress could do so, by its enactment of the McCarran Act. By it Congress declared that the continued regulation and taxation of insurance by the states was in the public interest, and that its silence should not be construed to interpose any barrier thereto. To make assurance doubly certain it expressly subjected insurance to the regulatory and tax laws of the states, and limited the effects of its own legislation relating to that business. The validity of this Act was sustained in *Prudential Insurance Company v. Benjamin.*[51] For purposes of deciding that case the Court assumed the state tax to be discriminatory to such an extent as would have rendered it invalid under the commerce clause had Congress remained silent. It is also assumed that the Company's entire business in the taxing state was interstate commerce, not merely something affecting such commerce. This gives to the decision the broadest possible scope and significance. It denies that the limits that have been imposed on state powers in the absence of affirmative legislation by Congress fix the limits of the latter's power to aid state policies. There had been previous intimations that Congress could free the states' taxing power from the limits

50. United States v Southeastern Underwriters Ass'n, (1944) 322 U.S. 533.

51. (1946) 328 U.S. 408.

imposed thereon by the commerce clause.[52] But this is the first to apply to that power the principles that had already been used in support of state regulatory legislation relating to intoxicants and prison-made goods.

There has been no decision on whether Congress may intervene to restrict the powers of the state as it may to expand them. It does, of course, actually do so whenever it validly regulates matters that a state may regulate in the absence of action by it. But would its action be valid if it took the form of a denial to the state of the power to enforce a regulation or impose a tax that would not transgress the limits placed on a state by the commerce clause itself apart from Congressional action? There have from time to time been broad statements that Congress has the power "to redefine the distribution of power over interstate commerce" by either permitting the states to regulate it "in a manner which would otherwise not be permissible" or excluding "state regulation even of matters of peculiarly local concern which nevertheless affect interstate commerce."[53] The logical implication of this premise would permit it to curb states' regulatory powers by legislation having that as its sole objective. Even stronger language has been used with respect to its power to limit the taxing powers of the states. Its power to intervene where the state taxes interstate commerce itself has been recognized by the Court.[54] But a more extreme position was taken in the *Northwest Airlines Case* which in-

52. See, for example, Gwin, White & Prince, Inc. v. Henneford, (1939) 305 U.S. 434, 438.
53. Southern Pacific v. Arizona, (1945) 325 U.S. 761, 769.
54. McGoldrick v. Berwind-White Coal Co., (1940) 309 U.S. 33, 49, 50. See also Freeman v. Hewit, (1946) 329 U.S. 249.

volved a tax on Airlines' entire fleet of planes imposed by its domiciliary state. The prevailing opinion of Justice Frankfurter stated that "Congress of course could exert its controlling authority over commerce by appropriate regulation and exclude a domiciliary State from authority which it otherwise would have because it is the domiciliary State."[55] But it remained for Justice Jackson, in his concurring opinion in that case, to carry this theory to its utmost limits. He says:

> "Congress has not extended its protection and control to the field of taxation, although I take it no one denies that constitutionally it may do so. It may exact a single uniform federal tax on the property or the business to the exclusion of taxation by the states. It may subject the vehicles or other incidents to any type of state and local taxation, or it may declare them tax-free altogether."[56]

He carries into this field a principle that has been sustained when Congress has sought to protect federal agencies and instrumentalities against state taxation. If these various expressions of the Court may be taken as an indication of what it would hold were it called upon to decide such an issue, then indeed will the commerce power have become a most serious potential threat to the states. That the Court would actually transform these dicta into law is highly probable.

The theory just stated has not yet been put to a practical test. While it cannot be ignored in appraising the effect that recent interpretations of the commerce clause have had upon state powers, it still is but one of the data for a generalization. The majority of the

55. N. W. Airlines, Inc. v. Minnesota, (1944) 322 U.S. 292, 298.
56. At pp. 303 and 304 of 322 U.S.

decisions since 1933 point in the opposite direction. The general trend has been towards an expansion of state powers by freeing them of some of the restraints thereon based upon implications from the commerce clause as construed prior to 1933. This trend has been increased by granting Congress a wider power to use its authority to grant relief from restrictions that only its action can remove. The net effect of the decisions has been well summarized by Justice Rutledge in his opinion in the *Prudential Insurance Company Case.* After calling attention to the oscillatory character of the interpretations of the commerce clause in both its affirmative and prohibitive aspects, he states:

> "For concurrently with the broadening of the scope for permissible application of federal authority, the tendency also has run toward sustaining state regulatory and taxing measures formerly regarded as inconsonant with Congress' unexercised power over commerce, and to doing so by a new, or renewed, emphasis on facts and practical considerations rather than dogmatic logistic. These facts are of great importance for disposing of such controversies. For in effect they have transferred the general problem of adjustment to a level more tolerant of both state and federal legislative action."[57]

The doctrine that the very existence of the federal system imposed certain implied limits on the states has had a long and varied career. It was first applied in *McCulloch v. Maryland*[58] to prevent that state from taxing the note issue power of the Second Bank of the United States, a private enterprise operating as an

57. Prudential Insurance Co. v. Benjamin, (1946) 328 U.S. 408.
58. (1819) 4 Wheat. 316.

instrumentality of the federal government. Despite certain language in Chief Justice Marshall's opinion therein which might have afforded a basis for limiting its scope to state action, the principle was subsequently extended to protect the states from federal action deemed to impede the performance of their functions.[59] By 1933 it had developed into a vast body of decision curtailing the taxing powers of both the states and the federal government.[60] There is no precise method for determining how far the numerous applications that had been given to this immunity principle actually benefited the governments it was intended to protect. No one doubted its immediate benefit to those whom it relieved of the payment of one tax or another. Whether in the long run it was of net benefit to them was another matter. Another obvious effect was a reduction of the tax sources available to the states and the nation. But again, whether or not there were compensating fiscal gains to offset such revenue losses might be difficult, if not impossible, to tell. In any event, the law had been developed without much, if any, reference to such considerations. New applications of the principle were being constantly made even after 1933. Since 1937 the trend has been definitely in the opposite direction. Not only has no extension been made, but several long established immunities have been eliminated.

The Court's revision of this principle has been largely determined by three factors. The first of these

59. Collector v. Day, (1871) 11 Wall. 113.
60. See Rottschaefer, Handbook on American Constitutional Law, Secs. 74–82.

was giving more and more weight to the restrictive effects of the immunity upon the taxing power of the government imposing the tax. Another was the tendency to determine whether or not the tax impeded the functioning of the other government by factual analysis rather than by a priori methods. An important element in this connection was the refusal to infer the existence of the prohibited burden merely from the fact that the tax increased the cost of the other government's performance of its functions. The last factor was an increased recognition that the major immediate benefits of the immunity accrued to private persons and thus relieved them of a burden borne by others without proof of compensating advantages to the government for whose benefit the immunity was granted. The task of establishing the immunity in a given case become more and more difficult for those asserting it. This became evident in *James v. Dravo Contracting Company*[61] which sustained a state tax on the gross earnings from construction contracts with the United States. The Court selected as decisive those precedents that supported the tax rather than those that would have condemned it. The Company had relied upon *Panhandle Oil Company v. Mississippi*[62] and *Graves v. Texas Company*.[63] These had invalidated state gasoline taxes on gasoline sold to federal agencies. They were summarily disposed of by being limited to their particular facts. That they have been in effect overruled is a fair inference from their treatment in *Alabama v. King &*

61. (1937) 302 U.S. 134.
62. (1928) 277 U.S. 218.
63. (1936) 298 U.S. 393.

Boozer.[64] This involved an Alabama sales tax on goods sold to a contractor constructing an army camp for the United States under the "cost plus fixed fee" basis. The tax, therefore, directly increased its cost and its final incidence would be on the United States. The tax as thus applied was held valid. This was said to be the normal incident of the existence of two independent governments operating within the same territory. It was denied that the right of the one government to be free from taxation by the other meant immunity from paying the added costs attributable to taxing those who furnish supplies to the former and who have been granted no tax immunity. The views that prevailed in the *Panhandle Oil Company* and the *Texas Company Cases* are said to be no longer tenable. The instant case did not involve a direct sale to the United States, or one of its agencies, as did the sales in those two cases. A tax on a direct sale would have no greater effect than that involved in the *King & Boozer Case.* Since that effect is described as one that may fairly be borne by the United States, it is reasonable to infer that the two cases referred to have been impliedly overruled. This would be in line with the trend shown by the express overruling of *Gillespie v. Oklahoma*[65] in *Helvering v. Mountain Producers Corporation,*[66] decided in 1938.

The inability of either government to tax the compensation received by the employees and officers of the other was an accepted principle both before 1933 and for several years thereafter. It had been twice used dur-

64. (1941) 314 U.S. 1.
65. (1922) 257 U.S. 501.
66. (1938) 303 U.S. 376.

ing 1937, once to invalidate a state income tax upon the salary of a federal official,[67] and once to defeat a federal tax upon that of a state employee.[68] Its scope was limited by two decisions rendered during 1938, both of which involved federal taxation of the compensation of state employees.[69] Neither, however, was based on an outright rejection of the entire principle. This occurred during 1939 when the Court sustained a state income tax upon the salary of counsel for the Home Owners' Loan Corporation, a wholly owned federal instrumentality.[70] It was assumed to be an agency through which the United States was exercising its strictly governmental functions. The theory was rejected that such a tax imposed an economic burden that was "in some way passed on so as to impose a burden on the national government tantamount to an interference by one government with the other in the performance of its functions." Since that had been the basis for the granting of this immunity, that could no longer stand. The Court makes it very clear that it intends to abolish the immunity completely, as well as the reciprocal immunity of the compensation of state employees and officers from federal income taxes. It is a most sweeping decision. Its principles may well be applied to destroy many tax immunities formerly deduced from the original principle so far as their immediate beneficiaries are private persons who have benefited from it with respect to their relations with government. But that it may not

67. New York ex rel. Rogers v. Graves, (1937) 299 U.S. 401.
68. Brush v. Com'r of Internal Revenue, (1937) 300 U.S. 352.
69. Helvering v. Gerhardt, (1938) 304 U.S. 405; Helvering v. Therrell, (1938) 303 U.S. 218.
70. Graves v. People ex rel. O'Keefe, (1939) 306 U.S. 466.

be construed to abolish all forms of the immunity is clear from the late decision in *United States v. Alleghany County*[71] which held that federally owned property may not be taxed by a state without the consent of the United States. The immunity is preserved to protect the federal government to the extent that the immediate incidence of the state tax is upon its property or its activities. Any discriminatory tax is still prohibited.

The net effect of these decisions has been to expand a state's taxing power by freeing it to some extent of a serious limit thereon. The principal undetermined issue in this field concerns the taxation of bonds issued by the United States and its instrumentalities, and the interest thereon. The states have had to pay a price for this new freedom in a correlative increase in the federal government's taxing power. Furthermore, no decision has protected them against having Congress intervene to deprive them of the advantages gained.[72] This it may do, even without similarly limiting the federal government's new powers attributable to recent revisions of the principle of inter-government tax immunity. This, however, cannot alter the fact that constitutional restrictions on their powers have been so redefined as to give them potentially greater scope.

The states' power to tax has also been expanded through redefining other constitutional limits upon it. The jurisdiction of states to tax had long been held limited by that provision of the Fourteenth Amendment

71. (1944) 322 U.S. 174.
72. The Federal Land Bank of St. Paul v. Bismarck Lumber Co., (1941) 314 U.S. 95.

prohibiting a state from depriving any person of property without due process of law. There is no linguistic technique by which there can be derived therefrom the proposition that state taxation of things, persons, or activities beyond its jurisdiction deprives anyone of property without due process of law. The result is achieved by postulating that the due process clause implies a policy to protect persons against unreasonable exercises of a state's taxing power. The problems of defining that policy, and determining when it is infringed by state action, leave much to the discretion of the Court. That discretion had been exercised in numerous cases involving many different kinds of tax. Present purposes do not require their consideration. It is sufficient to indicate that in at least one field of taxation, that of inheritance taxation, the Court had by 1933 defined the jurisdiction of a state so as to prevent multi-state inheritance taxation of the transfer of both tangible and intangible property.[73] The due process clause had been construed prior to 1930 to permit multi-state inheritance taxation of intangible personalty.[74] In that year the power to impose such tax on the transfer of bonds was limited to the state of the decedent's domicile.[75] The majority opinion shows clearly that the aim was to put an end to multi-state inheritance taxes. The doctrine was extended within the next two years to other kinds of intangible personalty, including corporate shares of stock.[76] This remained law

73. See Rottschaefer, Handbook of American Constitutional Law, Sec. 283.
74. Blackstone v. Miller, (1902) 188 U.S. 189.
75. Farmers Loan & Trust Co. v. Minnesota, (1930) 280 U.S. 204.
76. First Nat'l Bank of Boston v. Maine, (1932) 284 U.S. 312.

until 1939 when *Curry v. McCanless*[77] rejected the theory that multi-state inheritance taxes could never be validly imposed. It permitted it in circumstances in which decedent had so acted with respect to the intangibles as to have sought and received the protection of more than a single state for them and their transfer. Within four years thereafter the Court had expressly overruled the decision limiting to the state of decedent's domicile the taxation of the transfer of corporate shares by permitting the state of the corporate domicile to tax.[78] It had also overruled an earlier decision limiting the jurisdiction of the state of decedent's domicile under a state of facts that would clearly permit another state also to tax the transfer.[79] It has also confirmed such domiciliary state's power where another state also could tax, but this did not require any earlier decision to be overruled.[80] The taxpayer was relying upon the theory that one state only could tax under the circumstances of his case. The reasoning in all these later cases implicitly denies that due process limits inheritance taxes on the transfer of intangible personalty to one state. It is not intended merely to substitute another state for that of decedent's domicile under a "one state" rule. It is extremely doubtful that any of the decisions limiting such taxation to a single state are still law.

It is still undetermined whether multi-state property taxation of intangible personalty is valid. It probably is. The question was posed in *Newark Fire Insurance*

77. (1939) 307 U.S. 357.
78. State Tax Commission of Utah v. Aldrich, (1942) 316 U.S. 174.
79. Graves v. Schmidlapp, (1942) 315 U.S. 657, overruling Wachovia Trust Co. v. Doughton, (1926) 272 U S. 567.
80. Central Hanover Bk. & Tr. Co. v. Kelly, (1943) 319 U.S. 94.

Company v. State Board of Tax Appeals,[81] a case in which but eight of the Court's members sat. Four of them avoided the issue. The other four, who concurred in the result, based their decision on a principle which permitted multi-state taxation of such property. One of the former group, and three of the latter, are still on the Court. The views of the latter represent the law of today. It accords with what was the law prior to 1933, but at least the attempt to narrow state power to tax property failed. Multi-state income taxation of the same income was permitted with respect to most kinds of income even before 1933. Uncertainty existed only as to income from real property and tangible personalty. The jurisdiction of the state of their situs was admitted. It was a question whether the state of their owner's domicile would be permitted to tax. That it had jurisdiction to do so was decided in the *Cohn Case*.[82] A state's power to tax nonresidents received an extension that it would not have obtained prior to 1933 in *International Harvester Company v. Wisconsin Department of Taxation*.[83] The language in its opinion is so sweeping and vague that, if extended to other forms of taxation, it might entail whittling down the protection of the due process clause still further.

It is only in the field of state jurisdiction to tax that a clear case can be made for the proposition that recent decisions have expanded state taxing powers. The due process clause has not since 1920 interposed any serious obstacle to the purposes for which a state may levy

81. (1939) 307. U.S. 313
82. People ex rel. Cohn v. Graves, (1937) 300 U.S. 308.
83. (1944) 322 U.S. 435.

taxes. Nor has the equal protection clause of the Fourteenth Amendment restricted materially its freedom in determining how it will distribute its tax burden. In no instance has any decision since 1935 cut down its freedom in this respect. Hence, it may be concluded that the recent trend has been wholly in favor of expanding the scope of the states' taxing powers so far as these were limited by the due process and equal protection clauses of the Fourteenth Amendment. While it has been suggested that Congress might interpose to restrict their freedom, it has never been so held.

The purpose of the discussion in this Chapter was to discover the effect of recent judicial trends upon the regulatory and taxing powers of the states. That it has expanded their potential scope may be taken as beyond dispute. This does not mean that their powers today are greater than before 1933. There is no measure available for determining whether the shrinkage due to the expansion of federal powers is less than, equal to, or greater than, the expansion attributable to the reduction of the restrictive effects of certain limitations upon state powers. All that can be safely asserted is that the power of the states today is greater than it would have been but for the decisions considered in this Chapter. Some of this is due to a revision of such established doctrines as that of intergovernmental immunity. Some was the result of Congressional action. But, whatever the technique through which it was accomplished, these recent decisions have paved the way for a more extensive and intensive assertion of state power. The Supreme Court has, in this field also, interpreted the Constitution in accordance with the general trend towards increasing governmental control and activity.

IV

The Protection of Personal
And Property Rights

THE Constitution contains several provisions whose purpose is the protection of certain individual interests of person and property against governmental action. Some of these apply to the federal government, others to the states only. Some limit all branches of government, others restrict the legislative branch alone. The protection of individualism is thus an integral part of our constitutional system. Provisions especially relevant to our subject are the due process clause of the Fifth Amendment, the Thirteenth Amendment prohibiting involuntary servitude, the due process and equal protection clauses of the Fourteenth Amendment, and the contract clause of Article I, Section 10, of the original Constitution. The kinds of individual interest which they protect are many and diverse, but what follows will be chiefly concerned with individual economic interests. The due process and contract clauses are the most important from this point of view, especially so far as they limit the substance of law as distinguished from the procedures employed by government to execute its policies.

These several constitutional provisions have never been construed to confer complete freedom of individual action. It has always been recognized that there were certain interests, generally designated by the expression "social interests" whose protection justified some restriction upon the individual's use of his freedom. A large part of the law has always had that as its objective, and still has. Furthermore, this usually involves limiting one individual's freedom to safeguard some interest of another individual. The laws of property and contract, which are basic to the maintenance of the economic system of private enterprise, operate in that manner. Government regulation of business consists in prescribing rules to govern the exercise of the entrepreneur's powers, and generally is expected to affect the individual interests of those who depend upon the enterprise in one way or another. These effects occur whether the regulation expands or restricts those powers. This is equally true of regulations of individual conduct and activities that are not primarily economic in motivation and character. There has been for some time an increasing tendency to extend the service enterprises conducted by government. Each extension in practice curtails the power and freedom of some for the purpose of enchancing another's welfare. The taxing power also operates in this fashion. Its exercise involves the transfer of wealth from the taxpayers to the government which spends it for purposes from which there is seldom an equivalence between contribution made and benefit received. The conscious use of that power to effect a redistribution of the national income is an excellent example of this. The "social interest" denotes no more than an aggregate of individual interests arranged as of any given moment in an order of priorities determined by the then prevailing ideas of what constitutes the desirable social order. This social ideal is the fundamental postulate of the theory of social interests. It is implicit in the reasoning by which courts determine whether the governments of our constitutional system have exceeded the limits imposed upon them for the protection of individual freedom.

This analysis reveals that the real issue that confronts a court when called upon to apply the due process and contract clauses is between competing individual interests. This is almost self-evident in such a case as *Miller v. Schoene*[1] which sustained, against an objection based on the due process clause, a state statute that permitted the uncompensated destruction of ornamental red cedars on one man's property to save another's apple orchard from injury due to a disease with which the cedars were infected. The Court properly recognized that the state would have been making a choice between these interests if it had not passed the law as much as by enacting it. It stated that "When forced to such a choice the state does not exceed its constitutional powers by deciding upon the destruction of one class of property in order to save another which, in the judgment of the legislature, is of greater value to the public." It is equally present when a creditor is forced to postpone his rights under a mortgage securing his investment as required by the moratory legislation during the recent depression. The final choice between such competing interests would belong to the legislature were it not for the theory that the interpretation of these constitutional provisions is a judicial function. That

1. (1928) 276 U.S. 272.

very fact alters the process of selection. A legislature which is limited by such provisions should test its choice for conformity with that made by the constitution. However, since the final decision on what that constitutional policy is belongs to the courts, its views thereon can never be more than tentative. The courts are perforce required to determine finally the policies these constitutional provisions were intended to protect, and the conformity of the legislative policy therewith. Consequently the source of our knowledge about these matters is judicial decisions. The very formulation of the issue indicates that the courts cannot escape deciding questions of policy that involve their use of wide discretion. This is especially true when they are interpreting the constitutional limitations with which this discussion is concerned. But the choices they make are also between competing individual interests. Their decisions postulate a social ideal as implicit in these constitutional limitations. But that social ideal is also merely a particular ordering of a vast number of competing individual interests that cannot all be fully satisfied because ours is a world of limited space and resources and our society is composed of persons whose individual value scales manifest a great amount of diversity.

The task of the courts is thus of such character that its performance is bound to be affected by social, political and economic theories and philosophies. Experience proves that these are not static. It also shows that changes therein ultimately affect the judicial interpretations of these constitutional limitations on governmental powers. The values once deemed deserving the greatest protection are subordinated to others to which altered theories and circumstances have assigned a new and greater importance. The entrepreneur's freedom of initiative may be more and more restricted on the assumption that it will be possible to increase the economic security of some or all members of the nation by creating a more stable economic order. It is obvious to the most casual observer that these constitutional provisions have been subjected to a considerable reinterpretation since 1933. It is equally obvious that the trend has been to narrow their restrictive effects, when measured by what had gone before, especially with respect to certain fields of individual activity. To the extent that this has occured has the field of potential government regulation been expanded. This applies to both the states and the nation. There have been other areas in which the scope of these limitations has been expanded, thereby entailing a corresponding decrease in the area of valid governmental control. So far as this has involved the creation of restrictions operating on both the states and the federal government, there are individual activities free from all government regulation of certain kinds. The decisions that held peaceful picketing to be an exercise of freedom of speech which neither government might prohibit is an example of what is here meant. There was a time in our recent history when the fact that judicial interpretations of the Constitution produced areas of such immunity was deemed so grave a usurpation of power by the courts as to warrant heroic measures to remedy that evil. Congress rejected the means proposed to accomplish this result, but time in due course fashioned the instrument. But the result was not the disappearance of those areas of complete immunity but the destruction of some that previous decisions had established and the creation of new ones. Thus were the demands of progress satisfied. The plain truth is that the existence of such areas is the inevitable result of giving any limiting effects to those constitutional limitations that bind both the states and the federal government, at least so far as they are given the same interpretation and application. The only way of abolishing them is either to amend the Constitution to eliminate them without substituting others therefor, or to so construe them as to reduce their scope to less than infinitesimal dimensions.

The problems to which this Chapter will be devoted concern the disappearance of some of the old, and the appearance of new, areas of immunity from governmental regulation of one kind or another. It is the changes relating to the regulation of economic activities, whether of capital or labor, to which the major part of the discussion will be devoted. A large body of decisions had been developed prior to 1933 defining the limits imposed by the due process clauses in this field.[2] The great majority of these involved the due process clause of the Fourteenth Amendment. This was quite normal since the regulation of economic activities had been left largely to the states during almost the whole of the period in which these decisions were accumulating. It would be impossible to deduce from them any generalization not expressed in language too vague to be of much value as a basis for predicting the course

2. See Rottschaefer, Handbook of American Constitutional Law, Secs. 233-255 (due process), and Secs. 256-278 (contract clause).

of future decisions. Nevertheless analysis of the cases would not have been wholly futile. It had never been decided that there existed any businesses protected against every conceivable type of government control. No regulations were held invalid on any such basis. They were condemned because found to restrict individual freedom too severely and beyond what courts deemed reasonably necessary to protect some aspect of the general welfare. It was frequently stated that a state had a wide, but not unlimited, discretion in determining the character of its economic system and institutions. The limits under the due process clause of the Fourteenth Amendment were in fact influenced by the common law's preference for competition. Common law conceptions also played an important part in defining the field within which price control was sustained. The burden of proof was upon those who sought to extend it, and it was difficult, but not impossible, to meet that burden. The regulation of capital and labor relations was made more difficult by the weight given by the courts to the idea of freedom of contract.[3] But it proved impotent in the face of a wide disparity in bargaining power between employer and employee. The theory of vested rights played an important part in limiting legislative control over property. It is impossible to read the record made prior to 1933 without concluding that the particular theory of individualism known as laissez faire contributed much to give the due process clauses their pre-1933 content.[4] The coun-

3. See Roscoe Pound, "Liberty of Contract," 18 Yale Law Jour. 454 (1909).

4. See E. S. Corwin, "The Supreme Court and the Fourteenth Amendment," 7 Mich. Law Rev. 643 (1909); E. S. Corwin, "Due Process of Law

tervailing claims of the police power, that is, the claim of the states and the federal government to intervene to modify the effects of unrestricted individualism was recognized in both theory and fact. Not all government regulation was held to conflict with the due process clauses. The point is merely that reforms trenching on the individual's freedom of economic activity were confronted with a formidable body of constitutional law that made it difficult for them to obtain judicial approval.

The most enthusiastic advocate of economic freedom is not likely to be averse to enlisting government aid in promoting his own interests. It is only necessary for proof to refer to the protective tariff system. The same narrow particularism motivated certain recent state regulation of insurance companies. A Virginia statute forbade insurance and indemnity companies authorized to do business within it to make contracts of insurance or surety on property or persons within it except through regularly constituted resident agents. Such agents were entitled to receive the customary commissions, and prohibited from paying any nonresident agent or broker more than fifty percent thereof. The effect of this statute was correctly described in the dissenting opinion of Justice Roberts as compelling "an insurance company which is a citizen of another state, and which negotiates a contract of insurance with an agent or broker within such other state, to pay a resident of Virginia for a service not rendered by him, but rendered by another in another state." The device employed to insure this

before the Civil War," 24 Harv. Law Rev. 366, 460 (1911); R. E. Cushman, "The Social and Economic Interpretation of the Fourteenth Amendment," 20 Mich. Law Rev. 737 (1922).

result was to require the contract to be countersigned by a resident agent in order to make it valid as to local risks. Disobedience of this provision entailed fines or revocation of the license to operate within the state. The statute in effect required a redistribution of income by those producing it to those who had at best a minor part therein. It was held not to violate the due process clause of the Fourteenth Amendment despite its obvious result, and an almost equally obvious purpose to obtain that result.[5] A specious argument was advanced intended to relate the provision to the promotion of the general welfare of the state by increasing its control over foreign insurance companies and their local business. The division of the commissions was justified as an exaction intended to assure the active use of resident agents in achieving that objective through their servicing of the contracts. The following year the principle was extended to a statute prohibiting certain classes of insurance companies from writing policies on local risks unless written through local agents receiving, and required to retain, the full commission due.[6] These cases in substance sanction legislation that resembles nothing so much as a holdup. It is difficult to reconcile this with the decision in *Thompson v. Consolidated Gas Utilities Corporation.*[7] That involved a state oil pro-ration order whose effect was to deprive the company of the opportunity to supply its market in order to benefit competing producers. The facts showed that it could not be justified as a conservation

5. Osborn v. Ozlin, (1940) 310 U.S. 53.
6. Holmes v. Springfield Fire & Marine Ins. Co., (1941) 311 U.S. 606.
7. (1937) 300 U.S. 55.

measure. It was condemned as a "glaring instance of the taking of one man's property and giving it to another" without a "justifying public purpose." It is true that in the Virginia case the Court found such "justifying public purpose" by piling one assumption on another. The last of these cases was decided in 1937, but three years prior to the first. The path of those who enlist government aid to secure a redistribution of income on their behalf has been rendered much easier by judicial action. An adequate "justifying public purpose" should now be easily found.

The equal protection clause of the Fourteenth Amendment has seldom been so restrictively construed as the due process clause. The Court has generally granted the legislature a fairly broad discretion in making classifications in enacting laws under both its police and tax powers. There have been a few decisions, such as *Connolly v. Union Sewer Pipe Company*[8] and *Truax v. Corrigan*,[9] that have achieved distinction as examples of an opposite judicial attitude. As recently as 1937 a statute exempting mutual fire and casualty insurance companies from a requirement imposed upon their competitors was held to violate the equal protection clause.[10] The dissenting opinion of Justice Roberts was concurred in by Justices Brandeis, Stone, and Cardozo. One would have to be a very naive person indeed to accept that decision as law today. *Truax v. Corrigan* was very properly distinguished in *Senn v. Tile Layers*

8. (1902) 184 U. S. 540.
9. (1921) 257 U.S. 312.
10. Hartford Steam Boiler Inspection & Insurance Co. v. Harrison, (1937) 301 U.S. 459.

Protective Union,[11] but no one would doubt that the
dissenting opinions of Justices Holmes, Pitney, and
Brandeis in the former present the views on this issue
(and for that matter on the due process issue also decided therein) today. As for the *Connolly Case,* the
prevailing opinion in *Tigner v. Texas*[12] effectually overruled it when it stated that *"Connolly's* case has been
worn away by the erosion of time, and we are of
opinion that it is no longer controlling." That case involved an attack upon the Texas antitrust law exempting agricultural products and livestock in the
hands of the producer or raiser from its provision
making conspiracy to fix prices a crime. The opinion
definitely reveals a conscious attempt to adjust the
interpretation of the Fourteenth Amendment to changes
in policy evidenced in legislation recognizing the
differences between the economic problems of agriculture and other economic activities. These examples
suffice to show that the Court has practically accepted
as conclusive of the constitutional issue the legislative
judgment that a classification made in legislation for
the control of business is reasonable. This gives the
legislature a wide power to affect the competitive situation by relieving a favored group from burdensome
controls imposed on others in the same field of economic
activity. While that was not the situation in the *Tigner
Case,* the principles invoked are capable of applications
involving such results.[13]

11. (1937) 301 U.S. 468.
12. (1940) 310 U.S. 141.
13. A very recent case involved a Louisiana statute that limited the privilege of becoming an official pilot on the lower Mississippi to those who, in
addition to meeting other prescribed qualifications, had served an appren-

Prices perform important functions under any economic system. It is difficult to conceive of the successful operation of a predominantly private enterprise system unless the entrepreneur is permitted to determine his own price policies. There is a sound basis for protecting his power to do so if the purpose is to maintain that system. He was exercising it over a much larger area of economic activities than today when the validity of governmental price control came before the Court for the first time.[14] The demand for it originated with the consumers who objected to what were charged to be exorbitant prices. The major problem from *Munn v. Illinois* in 1877 to *Nebbia v. New York*[15] in 1934 concerned the fixing of maximum prices. The former of these decided that due process was not violated by a state statute regulating the price of grain elevation at commercial centers. The majority of the Court based its decision in part upon analogies found in the common law under which those who devoted their property to the public use subjected it thereby to public regulation requiring them to "take but reasonable toll." Such property was said to be affected with a public interest. As the policy was extended to additional businesses, the test was reformulated so as to subject to this form of control businesses affected with such an interest. This

---

ticeship under an official pilot. It was charged in the case that this system in practice limited the position to relatives and friends of those under whom the apprenticeship had to be served. The evident discrimination implicit in this system was held not to violate the equal protection clause. Kotch v. Bd. of River Port Comm'rs, etc., (1947) 330 U.S. 552, 67 S. Ct. 910. Although official pilots were state officials appointed by the Governor of Louisiana, four of the Justices dissented.

14. Munn v. Illinois, (1877) 94 U.S. 113.

15. (1934) 291 U.S. 502.

removed any implications that it was limited to cases in which the regulated subject was the use of property. A long series of decisions left it uncertain just how a business affected with a public interest was to be distinguished from one not so affected. The grant of a legal monopoly or other special privileges, the possession of a monopoly in fact, the existence of excessive competition among consumers and that the commodity or service belonged to the class of necessities, were all invoked to support the conclusion that a particular business had become affected with a public interest.[16] These reduced somewhat the vagueness of that expression, but still left sufficient room for differences of judicial opinion to render doubtful the validity of any extension of the field of government price control. There were situations in which it was sustained solely for the purpose of protecting a limited group from oppression and extortion by unscrupulous persons.[17] No attempt was made to subsume these cases under the "affectation with a public interest" category. The usual form of price control has been that in which a government agency has fixed the price. Some legislation has merely required sellers or buyers to maintain in every locality in which they sell or buy a commodity the price maintained therefor in another locality except for differences due to variations in transportation costs to or

16. See Rottscheafer, Handbook of American Constitutional Law, Secs. 241, 242; H. Rottschaefer, "The Field of Governmental Price Control," 35 Yale Law Jour. 438 (1926); W. H. Hamilton, "Affection with a Public Interest," 39 Yale Law Jour. 1089 (1930); R. L. Hale, "The Constitution and the Price System: Some Reflections on Nebbia v. New York," 34 Col. Law Rev. 401 (1934).

17. See, for example, Calhoun v. Massie, (1920) 253 U.S. 170, and Yeiser v. Dysart, (1925) 267 U.S. 540.

from such localities. These had been sustained only when justifiable as a means for combatting monopoly.[18] Prior to 1933 there were quite a number of economic activities subject to governmental price control of one form or another. The due process clauses had prevented their application to others. The fixing of maximum, or maximum and minimum, prices was still considered to be valid in exceptional cases only. The principles developed to define those exceptions were looked upon as quite different from those applicable to other forms of regulation.

This was the situation when the *Nebbia Case* was decided in 1934. It involved the validity under the due process clause of the Fourteenth Amendment of a New York statute so far as it permitted fixing a minimum retail price for milk. The basic assumption underlying the attack was that governmental price-fixing could not validly be applied to a business not affected with a public interest as that concept had been defined by prior decisions. The Court's majority admitted that the dairy industry was not a public utility in the accepted sense of that term, and that the factors usually relied upon to put a business into the class of these affected with a public interest were absent. That which the majority admitted was the basis of the minority's condemnation of the statute. The majority in effect rejected the whole theory of the limits imposed on governmental price control by the due process clauses which had been gradually developed during a period of more than fifty years. Its general ideas are redefined. "The state-

18. Central Lumber Co. v. So. Dakota, (1912) 226 U.S. 157; Fairmont Creamery Co. v. Minnesota, (1927) 274 U.S. 1.

ment that one has dedicated his property to a public use" is stated to be "merely another way of saying that if one embarks in a business which public interest demands shall be regulated, he must know regulation will ensue." The definition of the phrase "affected with a public interest" is revised out of existence. It is stated that it "can, in the nature of things, mean no more than that an industry, for adequate reasons, is subject to control for the public good." The validity of price control was made to depend wholly upon the reasonableness of the legislative judgment that it was an appropriate means for remedying what it was free to regard as an evil or obstacle to the public welfare. This would permit it whenever the "economic maladjustment is one of price." Such was the situation of the dairy industry in New York when this legislation was enacted. The provision sustained was but one part of a general policy of protecting the dairy industry by raising the prices of its products. Though the majority attempted to relate it to the welfare of the consumers, the statute's principal purpose was to maintain the prices paid the producers. Its provision authorizing the fixing of minimum prices to be paid to producers by dealers was sustained not long after the *Nebbia Case* was decided.[19] The dealer involved therein was subject at the same time to orders fixing minimum prices for both his purchases from producers and his sales to his customers. The market situation was such that his minimum selling price would almost certainly be the maximum as well. This dual system was held not to violate his rights under the due process clause. His alleged losses were

19. Hegeman Farms Corp. v. Baldwin, (1934) 293 U.S. 163.

held due not to the governmental price policy but to the risks of competition against which due process clauses afforded no protection.

The *Nebbia Case* has completely changed the Court's approach to the constitutional problem first before it in *Munn v. Illinois*. In no case since 1934 has it held invalid any extension of governmental price control. It has not wholly rejected the older tools. It may still use them where they furnish an adequate basis for upholding price control.[20] But the mere fact that they would not insure such result is no longer equivalent to a death sentence for a new experiment in governmental price-fixing. The federal government has come to the assistance of the dairy industry with a plan very similar in purpose and method to that of New York. It has applied it also to the bituminous coal industry. Both have been held not to violate the due process clause of the Fifth Amendment.[21] In neither instance was the Court's reasoning reminiscent of the days when that kind of regulation was generally limited to businesses affected with a public interest. Equally significant is the overruling of the decision in *Ribnik v. McBride*[22] by *Olsen v. Nebraska*.[23] The former had held violative of due process a statute prescribing maximum fees chargeable by private employment agencies. In its opinion in the latter the Court states that "The drift away from *Ribnik* v. *McBride* . . . has been so great that it can no longer be deemed a controlling authority." Subsequent

20. See, for example, Townsend v. Yoemans, (1937) 301 U.S. 441.
21. United States v. Rock Royal Co-op, Inc., (1939) 307 U.S. 533 (milk); Sunshine Anthracite Coal Co. v. Adkins, (1940) 310 U.S. 381 (coal).
22. (1928) 277 U.S. 350.
23. (1941) 313 U.S. 236.

decisions are said to "represent in large measure a basic departure from the philosophy and approach of the majority in the *Ribnik* case." The *Nebbia Case* discarded the test by which price control was limited to businesses affected with a public interest. The attempt of the operator of the agency to limit legislative price-fixing to cases in which competition has failed to protect the public interest was rejected as going to the wisdom, but not the constitutionality, of that policy. It is questionable whether the due process clauses of the Fifth and Fourteenth Amendments today interpose any obstacle to legislative price-fixing. Government control over the entrepreneur's price policies is practically complete as far as the federal Constitution is concerned. Prior decisions[24] that rate regulation of private carriers violated due process clauses can no longer stand. The *Nebbia Case* has already been held to have had that result.[25] Nothing in present theories limits it to direct price-fixing. It applies equally to legislation requiring sellers and buyers to maintain in all localities prices bearing certain relations to those voluntarily established by them in any given locality. The limit placed on that policy by *Fairmont Creamery Company v. Minnesota* may be considered discarded. The implications of this new attitude may well extend to other forms of regulation heretofore deemed limited to public utilities or businesses affected with a public interest. It is doubtful that *New State Ice Company v. Liebmann*[26] *is* law today.

24. Smith v. Cahoon, (1931) 283 U.S. 553.
25. Mississippi River Fuel Corp. v. Federal Power Commission, (C.C.A. 8, 1941) 121 Fed. (2d) 159.
26. (1932) 285 U.S. 262.

The owners of the elevators involved in *Munn v. Illinois* had contended that they were entitled to reasonable compensation for the use of their property "even though it be clothed with a public interest"; and that what was reasonable was a judicial, not a legislative, question. This was denied, and they were referred to the polls to protect themselves against an abuse of legislative power. This doctrine was gradually supplanted well before 1900 in favor of one entitling the railroads and other public utilities to a judicial review of the reasonableness of governmentally prescribed rates. Out of this grew the principle that the due process clauses invalidated confiscatory rates. In 1898, in *Smyth v. Ames*, [27] the Court gave its first full discussion of this matter and announced that rates would be confiscatory unless they permitted those required to observe them to earn a fair return on the fair value of the property devoted to the public use. From that time on the courts were plagued with the problem of valuation. It is not necessary for present purposes to trace the historical development of their attempts to solve it. In theory the Court never departed from the position that the ascertainment of fair value was a matter of judgment "having its basis in a proper consideration of all relevant facts." In practice it laid down some rather definite rules as to the kind of evidence that would have to be taken into account by the rate-making authorities in reaching their conclusion as to fair value. The formula announced in *Smyth v. Ames* was a strange congeries of factors that might well have made effective regulation impossible. Some of them were practically aban-

27. (1898) 169 U.S. 466.

doned within a relatively brief period after that decision
although they continued to exert an influence in connection with the issue of going value. By 1933 the two
methods of valuation that retained judicial approval
were the cost and cost of reproduction less depreciation
theories.[28] Valuations had been rejected that had ignored
the latter, although in one case a valuation based on
historical cost and which practically ignored cost of
reproduction was sustained where a large portion of
the plant was of recent construction.[29] It was completely
and explicitly ignored in *Lindheimer v. Illinois Bell Telephone Company*[30] because the Company's experience
and its financial history under the rates being attacked
were wholly inconsistent with an inference that those
rates were confiscatory.

The developments in this field since 1939 have been
both rapid and important. In *Driscoll v. Edison Light
& Power Company*[31] rates were sustained when found
to yield a fair return on a rate base at least equal to the
depreciated cost of reproduction of the Company's property. Then came two highly important decisions involving rates fixed by the Federal Power Commission.
The first of these was *Federal Power Commission v.*

28. On the valuation problem, see E. C. Goddard, "Public Utility Valuation," 15 Mich. Law Rev. 205 (1917); G. C. Henderson, "Railway Valuation
in the Courts," 33 Harv. Law Rev. 902, 1031 (1920); F. G. Dorety, "The
Function of Reproduction Cost in Public Utility Valuation and Rate
Making," 37 Harv. Law Rev. 173 (1924); H. Rottschaefer, "Valuation in
Rate Cases," 9 Minn. Law Rev. 211 (1925); J. C. Bonbright, "Economic
Merits of Cost and Reproduction Cost," 41 Harv. Law Rev. 593 (1928)
29. Los Angeles Gas & El. Corp. v. R.R. Commission of California, (1933)
289 U.S. 287.
30. (1934) 292 U.S. 151.
31. (1939) 307 U.S. 104.

Natural Gas Pipe Line Company.[32] The statute under which the Commission acted expressly provided for judicial review of its rate orders, but its findings of fact were made conclusive if supported by substantial evidence. The principal opinion construed the standard for rates which the Commission was to follow as coinciding with that required by the Constitution. It sustained the rates which the Commission had fixed so as to allow a fair return on a rate base equal to the undepreciated cost of reproduction of the property as computed by the Company itself. This opinion made no contribution to clarifying the matter of determining the constitutionally required rate base. The views of Justices Douglas, Murphy, and Black are set forth in an opinion by the last named. It is a vigorous attack on *Smyth v. Ames* and the entire theory that the courts are authorized to set aside rates fixed by the legislature or by its authority merely because they fail to meet the judicial standard of reasonableness. It demands a return to the views of Chief Justice Waite in *Munn v. Illinois*, and would restrict judicial review to securing compliance with the procedural requirements of due process. The same views had been expressed by these Justices and Justice Frankfurter in cases decided a few years before.[33] While this point of view has not yet been formally accepted as law, the need for that has been greatly reduced, if not eliminated, by the subsequent decision in *Federal Power Commissiom v. Hope Natural Gas Company.*[34]

32. (1942) 315 U.S. 575.

33. See McCart v. Indianapolis Water Co., (1938) 302 U.S. 419, and Driscoll v. Edison Lt. & Pr. Co., (1939) 307 U.S. 104.

34. (1944) 320 U.S. 591. See R. L. Hale, "Utility Regulation in the Light of the Hope Natural Gas Case," 44 Col. Law Rev. 488 (1944); John Bauer,

In arriving at the order before the Court, the Commission had taken as the rate base the "actual legitimate cost" of the Company's property used to furnish the gas whose rates were in issue. The majority opinion stated that the Commission was under no duty to use any single formula or combination of formulae in determining rates, since its orders were to be tested by their results and not by the method employed to reach them. An analysis of the Company's financial history served to base the conclusion that the result could not be condemned as unjust to either the investor or consumer. Hence there was no need to discuss the various methods of computing the rate base. The issue before the Court was that of construing the statute under which the Commission acted. However, the opinion expressly states that "Since there are no constitutional requirements more exacting than the standards of the Act, a rate order which conforms to the latter does not run afoul of the former." The decision may accordingly be taken to represent the Court's view that regulatory bodies do not violate due process clauses by using prudent investment as the rate base so far as that is still a factor. But the ultimate basis for the decision was that rates could not be held unjust or unreasonable that enabled the Company "to operate successfully, to maintain its financial integrity, to attract capital, and to compensate its investors for the risks assumed . . . even though they might produce only a meager return on the so-called 'fair value' rate base." This is in substance

---

"The Establishment and Administration of a 'Prudent Investment' Rate Base," 53 Yale Law Jour. 495 (1944).

the test used to sustain the rates in *Lindheimer v. Illinois Bell Telephone Company.*

It is worth noting that the majority opinion merely states that rates that meet the test just set forth cannot be said to be invalid. Logically this is not equivalent to an assertion that rates must satisfy it in order to be valid. That there may well be situations in which rates will be sustained though not permitting a fair return on investment is probable. The rate-making process is described as one involving a balancing of investor and consumer interests. The same view had been expressed in Justice Black's concurring opinion in the *Natural Gas Pipeline Company Case.* In his statement he adds that "The investor and consumer interests may so collide as to warrant the rate-making body in concluding that a return on historical cost or prudent investment, though fair to investors, would be grossly unfair to the consumers." He does not state whose interests shall prevail in such a situation, but there is no doubt whatever that it would not be the investor's. Such was the solution adopted when the old "fair value" rule of *Smyth v. Ames* prevailed. The results of such a policy might be disastrous to the private operation of public utilities under a regime in which the rate base was measured by prudent investment. But one rate case has been decided by the Court since the *Hope Natural Gas Company Case.* Rates were sustained that were arrived at by taking as the rate base an amount less than investment but equal to the price at which the Company had offered to sell its street railway system to San Francisco.[35] This special

35. Market Street Ry. Co. v. R. R. Commission of California, (1945) 324 U.S. 548.

feature limits the value of the decision, but it may well be that the rates would have been sustained though the Company had not indicated its own views of the worth of its properties by its offer to sell. It was in a failing condition and in an industry for whose services the demand was shrinking. It would probably come within Justice Black's principle for preferring the interests of consumers to those of investors, especially since the latters' losses were ultimately due to general economic changes affecting the industry.

All of the cases dealing with the valuation problem as an element in determining whether rates prescribed by the public were confiscatory involved public utilities or services that had been analogized to them. All also involved maximum rates. Some had been directly fixed by the legislature, others by administrative boards in accordance with a legislatively fixed standard. In the former case there would have been practically no possibility of prescribing rates adapted to the special circumstances of each person subjected to them. This was possible in the latter case. The federal legislation which authorized price and rent control during the war was executed by an administrator in accordance with standards laid down by Congress. These did not require rents to be fixed which would be fair in each particular case. It was necessary only that they should be generally fair and equitable, with procedures available to landlords for obtaining relief in hardship cases. The right to enforce the general standard in individual cases in which the permissible rent would not permit the landlord to earn a fair return on the fair market value of his property was litigated in the lower federal courts but received no extensive discussion from the Supreme Court. The decisions denied that the due process clause of the Fifth Amendment guaranteed that right.[36] The analogy of the cases in which it had been held to exist were held not to be relevant. The principal affirmative reasons urged in support of the position were the temporary character of the regulation, the fact that this was of much shorter duration than the useful life of housing accommodations, the fact that the landlord was not required to continue in the business, and the administrative impossibility of effectuating the objectives of rent control were that limit to apply. The same considerations could be used to sustain the same policy with respect to the other federal price controls during the war. Some would justify it regardless of the source of the emergency. Nor can their scope be confined to federal control but includes state regulation as well. No other limits are suggested.

It is a fair question whether there exist today any limits on the prices that government may fix in a field in which price regulation is constitutionally permissible. The decision in the *Hope Natural Gas Company Case* did not decide that there were none. It only held that the limit, if any, had not been violated by what the Commission did in that case. Nor is it a necessary implication therefrom that none exist. It is certain that for some time to come the only effective limit will be one established by the legislature or determined by a new judicial standard developed in the course of court review of administrative rate orders. The doctrine of

36. See especially the discussion in Wilson v. Brown, (Em. Ct. App. 1943) 137 Fed. (2d) 348.

the *Ben Avon Case*[37] lost some of its force as a result of the decision in the *St. Joseph Stock Yards Case*.[38] It has now lost whatever importance that decision left it since the "constitutional facts," which it assumes, have ceased to be such. The situation demands a vigorous judicial enforcement of all the procedural requirements of due process. This includes not only insuring a fair and complete hearing before the administrative agencies charged with fixing rates and other prices, but an effective review to determine whether their orders are supported by the evidence introduced at the hearings and which those affected by the order have had an adequate opportunity to meet. There is evident today no trend towards relaxing the requirements for a fair hearing,[39] but there is a definite trend on the part of courts to accept the fact findings of administrative agencies and to hold their orders supported by the record. This procedural protection is of no avail when the legislature itself fixes rates or other prices. The protection of those affected thereby either has been reduced to a minimum or is nonexistent. It is also difficult to translate constitutional limitations into effective protection of persons affected by price control of the kind prevailing during the war. The expansion of the field of permissible price control may produce many situations in which that method will be the only practicable one if the legislative price policy is to operate successfully. The result of recent developments in the field of governmental price control has been not only to severely

37. Ohio Valley Water Co. v. Ben Avon Borough, (1920) 253 U.S. 287.
38. St. Joseph Stockyards Co. v. United States, (1936) 298 U.S. 38.
39. See, for example, Ohio Bell Tel. Co. v. Ohio Pub. Util. Commission, (1937) 301 U.S. 292, and Morgan v. United States, (1938) 304 U.S. 1.

limit the scope of the entrepreneur's former constitutional freedom of action, but also to increase greatly his risks in carrying on his economic activities.

The regulation of the relations of capital and labor is an ancient problem. Its difficulties have varied directly with the increasing industrialization of the nation. During the greater part of the period while the nation was going through the transition from a predominantly agricultural economy to one predominantly industrial, the states were the source of the major part of the legislation regulating these relations. This occurred after the Fourteenth Amendment was adopted. Its due process clause became the principal obstacle to such legislation. It was successfully invoked to invalidate most of it that limited the hours of labor. It is only necessary to refer to *Lochner v. New York.*[40] Each new form of regulation was assailed as depriving both employer and employee of the freedom of contract guaranteed him by this clause. Despite this, much legislation was sustained prior to 1933 against objections based thereon.[41] This included such important measures as employers' liability and workmen's compensation acts. Minimum wage laws and legislation for the protection of trade unionism were conspicuous examples of the continuing force of due process clauses. The extent of their revision by judicial decision since 1933 can be most readily demonstrated by considering decisions involving recent legislation relating to these matters.

Minimum wage laws are one form of price-fixing

40. (1905) 198 U.S. 45.
41. See Rottschaefer, Handbook of American Constitutional Law, Sec. 243.

legislation. It was viewed by courts in the same manner as were other forms of price control, something violative of due process clauses in other than exceptional cases. It continued to be so considered though much legislation regulating the time and method of wage payment was sustained. The first instance in which it was held valid by the Supreme Court involved the Adamson Act enacted by Congress in 1916 to meet the threat of a general railway strike. It established the standard workday at eight hours as a permanent policy, prohibited the reduction of wages during a prescribed period but not permanently, and required payment for overtime at the resulting new hourly rate. Since the standard at the time was a ten-hour day, this necessarily fixed wages for the limited period prescribed. The Court recognized this and dealt with the Act on that basis. In sustaining it the temporary and emergency character of the measure was emphasized.[42] The decision was in no sense authority that the due process clauses permitted the general regulation of the wages of adults, or for that matter, of minors. It was six years after this decision that the validity of general wage legislation received its first extended discussion by the Court in the *Adkins Case*.[43] The District of Columbia minimum wage law enacted by Congress was therein held to violate the due process clause of the Fifth Amendment so far as it applied to adult women employees. The Court's majority deemed it an unreasonable restriction upon the freedom

42. Wilson v. New, (1917) 243 U.S. 332. See T. R. Powell, "The Supreme Court and the Adamson Law," 65 U. of Pa. Law Rev. 607 (1917).

43. Adkins v. Children's Hospital of Dist. of Columbia, (1923) 261 U.S. 525. See T. R. Powell, "The Judiciality of Minimum Wage Legislation," 37 Harv. Law Rev. 545 (1924).

of contract of both the employer and employee. The decisive factor was that the Act did not require the wages fixed to bear any relation to the earning power of the employee, and that the standard set took account only of the necessities of the employee. The Court's minority believed it to be valid under prior decisions and because the legislative judgment that it would produce certain desirable objectives was not unreasonable.

The first case involving such legislation after 1933 was *Moorhead v. New York*,[44] decided in 1936. The New York statute had been carefully framed to meet the factors relied upon to invalidate the Act before the Court in the *Adkins Case*. It expressly required the wages fixed to take into account the value of the services as well as the need of women employees for a living wage. Despite this difference, the law was held an undue interference with freedom of contract. The decision is based in part only on the fact that the employee's necessities were to figure in fixing the wage-rate. Its ultimate basis was that the state was "without power by any form of legislation to prohibit, change or nullify contracts between employers and adult women workers as to the amount of wages to be paid." That effectively foreclosed any legislative wage-fixing for any workers with the possible exception of minors and those paid under contracts to which a state or the Nation was a party. The majority's fear that sustaining the legislation because of changed conditions since the *Adkins Case* would open the way for upholding wage-fixing for adult males influenced it in rejecting that argument. While the dissent of Chief Justice Hughes

44. (1936) 298 U.S. 587.

was partly based on the fact that the New York statute recognized the importance of factors ignored by the Act held invalid in the *Adkins Case*, Justice Stone rested his dissent on the broader ground that the statute was reasonably necessary to obviate the consequences of the disparity in bargaining power between employer and employee.

The theory of Justice Stone would sustain wage regulation in practically every case. It was a principal consideration in the decision in *West Coast Hotel Company v. Parrish*,[45] rendered in 1937, which sustained a minimum wage law as applied to adult women. The statute was similar in its terms to that involved in the *Adkins Case* which it expressly overruled. The decision was also supported by the economic argument that low wages force states to subsidize unscrupulous employers and thus burden the public. The due process clause was held not to require them to do so. Liberty of contract was redefined to mean "liberty in a social organization which requires the protection of law against the evils which menace the health, safety, morals and welfare of the people." It is "necessarily subject to the restraints of due process, and regulation which is reasonable in relation to its subject and is adopted in the interests of the community is due process." The *New York* and *West Coast Hotel Company Cases* were both 5 to 4 decisions. Justice Roberts was a member of the majority in each of them. All of the cases, except that involving the Adamson Law, involved minimum wages for adult women only. A few years after the *West Coast Hotel Company Case*, the Court sus-

45. (1937) 300 U.S. 379.

tained the minimum wage provisions of the Fair Labor Standards Act which applied to minors and adults, to men as well as to women.[46] The only reason adduced to support this position was that "Since our decision in *West Coast Hotel Co. v. Parrish,* ... it is no longer open to question that the fixing of a minimum wage is within the legislative power and that the bare fact of its exercise is not a denial of due process under the Fifth more than under the Fourteenth Amendment." Whether due process imposes any limits on the level at which minima may be set has never been decided. It was only in *Wilson v. New* that the Court adverted to the problem of confiscation. It said that "it is always to be borne in mind that as to both carrier and employee the beneficent and ever-present safeguards of the Constitution are applicable and therefore both are protected against confiscation . . ." This was probably intended to be limited to common carriers and other public utilities, and not to be applicable to businesses not under their special duty to serve the public. But however wide its intended scope, its precise meaning is far from clear. It is unlikely that the Court will assume that task just after it has rid itself of the much simpler one of guarding public utility properties against confiscatory rate regulation. It will most likely permit the normal economic forces to run their course.

The reasoning by which general minimum wage laws were sustained rested on two assumptions as to what economic justice required. The first was the need to correct what was viewed as a maldistribution of income due to the disparity in bargaining power between em-

46. United States v. Darby, (1941) 312 U.S. 100.

ployer and employee. The second was the desire to shift to industry the cost necessary to permit the maintenance of a minimum standard of living for its employees. It was these elements in the general welfare that such legislation was intended to promote. The latter of these was also the motive back of the movement for unemployment and old age insurance and retirement pensions. Though the last of these received a temporary setback in 1935 when the Federal Railroad Retirement Act was held to violate the due process clause of the Fifth Amendment because of several of its important features,[47] social security systems, both federal and state, have been sustained against both due process and equal protection objections. The Retirement Act approached the problem through an exercise of the federal commerce power. The other forms of social security were established by a co-operative exercise of federal and state taxing powers. It is doubtful that the Railroad Retirement Act decision is still law. Another decision involved an order of the Interstate Commerce Commission that had back of it the same general purpose as social security legislation. The order authorized one railroad company to lease another's railroad property but required it to comply with certain terms intended to distribute part of the savings of the new operating arrangement to those workers who would incur financial loss from its being put into effect. Such losses included salary reductions incident to seniority shifts affecting retained employees, partial compensation for limited periods of those who lost their jobs due to the change, reimbursement of the moving expenses

47. Railroad Retirement Bd. v. Alton R. Co., (1935) 295 U. S. 330.

of employees transferred to new locations, and losses incurred by the latter group from forced sales of their homes. The Court could perceive no denial of due process in conditioning the grant of a valuable privilege to the lessee railroad on its using a part of its gains to compensate those suffering losses because of its exercise of the privilege.[48] It expressly supported its position by invoking the principle that a "business may be required to carry the burden of employee wastage incident to its operation" which underlies workmen's compensation laws. The analogy is a close one, but it is doubtful that such regulations would have been held valid in the nineteen-twenties. The decision itself would furnish a strong precedent for holding not violative of due process legislation requiring employers to compensate laid-off or discharged employees by some form of severance pay. It might even be extended to validate other compulsory payments by employers to their unorganized or organized employees. There is no reason to believe that the principle is limited by the special facts of the *Lowden Case*. The citation of workmen's compensation cases militates against any such attempt. This little-known decision may yet prove one of the most important in the recent line favorable to labor.

An important feature of present day governmental policy in the field of labor relations is encouraging and promoting the growth of labor unions. Earlier attempts to protect them by penalizing employers for dismissing workers because of union membership, or for requiring employees to sign "yellow dog" contracts, had been frustrated by the decisions in the *Adair* and *Coppage*

48. United States v. Lowden, (1939) 308 U.S. 225.

Cases[49] that such legislation interfered with the employer's liberty of contract guaranteed by the due process clauses of the Fifth and Fourteenth Amendments, respectively. Both decisions recognized the right of the individual worker to join unions, but denied that government could confer upon him the right to do so and still insist upon remaining in the employ of an employer unwilling to hire or retain union men. The last of these decisions was rendered in 1915. In 1926 Congress enacted the Railway Labor Act of 1926.[50] This required the representatives of the parties to an industrial dispute to be designated by them without interference, influence, or coercion by the other party. It was held to deny the employer no right protected by the applicable due process clause though it prevented him from fostering a company union.[51] This was the beginning of the active intervention of the federal government on behalf of trade unionism. It was motivated by the desire to promote industrial peace in interstate transportation.

It was not until after 1933 that it extended the area of economic activities within which it assumed to regulate labor relations. At the same time it intensified the degree of its regulation in this field. The National Labor Relations Act[52] conferred upon employees within its scope the rights of self-organization and collective bargaining, prohibited employers from interfering

49. Adair v. U. S., (1908) 208 U.S. 161; Coppage v. Kansas, (1915) 236 U.S. 1.
50. Act of May 20, 1926, Chap. 347, 44 Stat. 577; U.S.C., Title 45, Chap. 8
51. Texas & N. O. R. Co. v. Brotherhood of Ry. & S.S. Clerks, (1930) 281 U.S. 548.
52. Act of July 5, 1935, Chap. 372, 49 Stat. 449; U.S.C., Title 29, Chap. 7.

therewith, and denied them the right to engage in certain defined practices intended to encourage or discourage union membership. An amendment of the Railway Labor Act of 1926 in effect extended to employees covered by that Act similar provisions not originally a part thereof.[53] The former statute has been invariably sustained when any of its provisions have been questioned. The opinions in those cases contain very little, if any, discussion of due process aspects of the Act and its enforcement. The reasoning supporting the power of Congress to enact it apparently was deemed adequate also to dispose of due process objections thereto. The amendment of the Railway Labor Act of 1926 was held not to violate due process in requiring railroads to bargain collectively with the certified representatives of their employees.[54] The sanctions that may be imposed upon employers for the protection of labor's right to organize are largely left to the discretion of those who administer these Acts. The freedom of contract of employers covered by these Acts has been greatly curtailed. The rights of workers to organize is protected by methods condemned as violative of due process in the *Adair* and *Coppage Cases*. As stated in *Phelps Dodge Corporation v. N.L.R.B.*,[55] "The course of decisions in this Court since *Adair* v. *United States* . . . and *Coppage* v. *Kansas* . . . have completely sapped those cases of authority." That course of decision permits not only what those cases prohibited, but

53. Act of June 21, 1934, Chap. 691, 48 Stat. 1185; U.S.C., Title 45, Chap. 8.

54. Virginian Ry. Co. v. System Federation, No. 40, etc., (1937) 300 U.S. 515.

55. (1941) 313 U.S. 177.

so much more, that the employer's freedom of contract possesses about as much reality as did the right of labor to organize under the conditions existing in the *Coppage Case*.

The strike is organized labor's ultimate resort. Picketing, peaceful or otherwise, is one of the weapons usually employed to win a strike. The labor injunction was for long the employer's principal defensive weapon. It was one of labor's chief grievances against the courts. Its efforts to limit their power to issue it in labor disputes finally succeeded when Congress enacted the Norris-LaGuardia Act and many states passed similar laws. The validity of such legislation is now generally recognized at least when the limits imposed on the issuance of injunctions are no more restrictive than those found in the federal act. Some of the Supreme Court's reasoning in *Truax v. Corrigan*[56] indicated that such legislation would be held violative of the due process and equal protection clauses of the Fourteenth Amendment if enacted by the states, and the due process clause of the Fifth Amendment if enacted by Congress. But this proved unavailing against the trend when the issue came before the courts. Not all states prohibit injunctions merely because a labor dispute is involved. The due process clause of the Fourteenth Amendment has been construed to impose a limit where such statutes are not available, although a much narrower one than they afford. The first important case revealing the new trend involved a state statute which authorized giving publicity to labor disputes, declared peaceful picketing and patrolling lawful, and forbade injunc-

56. (1921) 257 U.S. 312.

tions prohibiting such conduct. The employer, who had a small contracting business, had refused to unionize his shop solely because he declined to subscribe to its rule which would have prevented him from working on his own jobs. He himself was ineligible for membership in the union. He sued to enjoin the peaceful picketing of his jobs by the union. He was in effect defending his right to work against interference by a private group whose claims conflicted therewith. The end sought by the union was the protection of the interests of its members against the harmful effects of the employers' acts. The rule to which he objected was deemed a reasonable means to that end. The harm to him was described as not due to any illegal action.[57] A state statute permitting peaceful picketing to inflict an injury of the kind suffered by the employer for the benefit of those responsible for the injury was held not prohibited by the due process clause of the Fourteenth Amendment. The clause was stated not to transform the employer's claim to work in his own business into a right guaranteed thereby against state action permitting other private persons or groups to prevent it as an incident to the promotion of their own interests by lawful means. It permits the state, at least within those limits, to prefer the interests of labor over those of the employer when these conflict. That this case would have been decided differently had it arisen prior to 1933 seems highly probable. The four so-called conservative Justices expressed their dissent in an opinion reflecting the views of the earlier period.

57. Senn v. Tile Layers Protective Union, (1937) 301 U.S. 468.

The Court in the case just discussed compared peaceful picketing by labor to advertising by businessmen. It had no occasion to determine its constitutional status since the state was authorizing, not prohibiting, it. Not until four years later was it held to be an exercise of freedom of speech and press that constitutes part of the liberty protected against hostile state action by the due process clause of the Fourteenth Amendment. The opinion of Justice Murphy in *Thornhill v Alabama*,[58] the first case to announce this doctrine, is an eloquent exposition of the importance of these values in a free society. His reason for including peaceful picketing in those categories is that "In the circumstances of our times the dissemination of information concerning the facts of a labor dispute must be regarded as within that area of free discussion that is guaranteed by the Constitution." The circumstances adduced all imply the need for the protection of the interests of labor and thereby the general public interest. The stress is on the need to inform the public. Were these considerations to be deemed pertinent in defining the limits of freedom of speech and press in relation to labor and capital relations, they might furnish a basis for restricting the employer's right to make his views thereon known to his own employees.

The problem that has confronted the Court since the

58. (1940) 310 U.S. 88. For a general discussion of the problem of the status of picketing as free speech, see Ludwig Teller, "Picketing and Free Speech," 56 Harv. Law Rev. 180 (1943); E. M. Dodd, Jr., "Picketing and Free Speech: A Dissent," 56 Harv. Law Rev. 513 (1943); Ludwig Teller, "Picketing and Free Speech: A Reply," 56 Harv. Law Rev. 532 (1943). On the general subject of the Supreme Court and labor, see E. M. Dodd, Jr., "The Supreme Court and Organized Labor," 58 Harv. Law Rev. 1018 (1945).

Thornhill Case has been to define the limits of this doctrine. It expressly stated therein that it was not concerned with mass picketing or other methods that might involve imminent danger to the public peace and safety. The next case[59] to reach the Court involved a labor dispute that had been marked by considerable violence on the part of the union conducting the strike. An injunction that included a prohibition of peaceful picketing among its terms was held not violative of due process because such picketing was "enmeshed with contemporaneously violent conduct which is concedely outlawed." The ultimate basis for a state's power to prohibit peaceful picketing is that past violence renders recurrence of violence on the picket line probable with the result that picketing would be a form of coercion rather than persuasion. As the majority opinion put it, "Nor can we say that it was written into the Fourteenth Amendment that a state through its courts cannot base protection against future coercion on an inference of the continuing threat of past misconduct." The Court divided sharply on this issue, but the majority's limitation would appear to be the minimum protection to which the public is entitled. There is as much reason for enjoining even peaceful picketing under such circumstances as for prohibiting violent picketing under such circumstances, and that has been sustained. But mere isolated acts of prior violence or abuse falling short of violence will not bring a case within the principle permitting enjoining peaceful picketing. Nor can the right be limited to employees

59. Milk Wagon Drivers Union, etc. v. Meadowmoor Dairies, Inc., (1941) 312 U.S. 287.

of the employer being picketed.[60] To limit it thus would prevent its use in attempts to unionize nonunion plants. The only other present limitation developed out of an attempt to force the owner of a café to compel a contractor constructing a building for the former to employ union labor only.[61] The building was being constructed a considerable distance from the café. It was only picketing of the café that had been enjoined. The majority adopted the view that picketing is as much subject to reasonable regulation as are other forms of free speech, and that a state may confine its sphere to that directly related to the dispute. While the language of some of the opinions intimates that false bannering might be validly prohibited, no case has yet so held.[62] It should be noted that there have been vigorous dissents in each case which has put limits on the right of peaceful picketing. Justices Black, Douglas, Murphy, and Reed seem bent on protecting this form of free speech with small regard to other public interests.

The liberal treatment extended to picketing is in marked contrast with that received by the employer's right to inform his employees of his views on unions and the facts of a labor controversy to which he is a party. It had been held in a case, decided after the *Thornhill Case,* that the Constitution did not impose on government with respect to purely commercial advertising the same restraints that protect the freedom of communicating ideas and disseminating opinion.[63] This is a perfectly reasonable position. That the Court has

60. A.F. of L. v. Swing, (1941) 312 U.S. 321.
61. Carpenters Joiners Union, etc. v. Ritters Cafe, (1942) 315 U.S. 722.
62. Cafeteria Employees Union, etc. v. Angelos, (1943) 320 U.S. 293.
63. Valentine v. Christensen, (1942) 316 U.S. 52.

not construed it as based on a general exclusion of business and economic activities from the protection that freedom of speech extends to the discussion of religious and political subjects is definitely asserted in *Thomas v. Collins*.[64] The employer's right to state his side of a labor dispute or his views on unions to both the public and his own employees has received formal recognition from the Court in several cases.[65] But at the same time it stated that this right would not be protected if the circumstances under which it was exercised gave the course of conduct of which it was a part the character of coercion. An excellent statement of this matter is found in the concurring opinion of Justice Douglas in *Thomas v. Collins*, where he says:

"No one may be required to obtain a license in order to speak. But once he uses the economic power which he has over other men and their jobs to influence their action, he is doing more than exercising the freedom of speech protected by the First Amendment. That is true whether he be an employer or employee. But as long as he does no more than speak he has the same unfettered right, no matter what side of an issue he espouses."[66]

The employer's right in this respect is thus limited by the same principle invoked to sustain the prohibition of peaceful picketing when the facts of the specific case justify the inference that the picketing will involve coercion and intimidation. The employer could not reasonably object to such a limitation if the safeguards to establish his use of the right as a means for coercion

64. (1945) 323 U.S. 516.
65. See, for example, N.L.R.B. v. Virginia El. & Pr. Co., (1941) 314 U.S. 469.
66. At pp. 543 and 544 of 323 U.S.

were as effective as those available to labor for that purpose. In the *Meadowmoor Dairies Case* the Court reserved for itself "the ultimate power to search the records in the state courts where a claim of constitutionality is effectively made." It did state that it was no part of its function to "make an independent evaluation of the testimony" before the state court, and that the latter's determination should be rejected only if it could be said to be "so without warrant as to be a palpable evasion of the constitutional guarantee" of free speech. The cases in which curtailment of the employer's right has been alleged have generally involved orders of the National Labor Relations Board. The statute under which it acts gives conclusive effect to its findings of fact "if supported by evidence," and thus precludes an independent judicial consideration thereof. So-called "constitutional facts" are not exempted from the statutory rule. The likelihood that the Court will set aside the Board's findings of fact as to the coercive effects of an employer's language is less under the statutory formula than that it will find a state court to have transgressed the vague test adopted in the *Meadowmoor Dairies Case.* It requires something more than a formal rule to achieve actual equality between employer and employee in this matter. The recent movement to curb the Board's power to throttle the employer's freedom of speech had considerable factual justification. It reflected also dissatisfaction with the failure of the courts to protect that right against the Board's aggression.

The latest aspect of government intervention in the field of labor relations is in sharp contrast with the

186 THE CONSTITUTION AND SOCIO-ECONOMIC CHANGE

policy pursued immediately after 1933. The emphasis
has shifted from fostering unions to their regulation.
Only a few of these regulations have thus far been passed
on by the Supreme Court. *Thomas v. Collins* [67] involved
a Texas statute which, as construed by the state court,
required a paid union organizer to procure a registration card from a state official before soliciting members
for his organization. Thomas, the president of the
International Union U.A.W., was found guilty of contempt of court for violating an injunction issued to
enforce the statute. The act of contempt consisted in
addressing a meeting held as part of an organizational
drive to unionize the employees of a certain industry,
in the course of which he issued both a general invitation
to join the union and one directed to a specific individual present in the audience. The majority and minority
of the Court disagree as to which of these acts constituted the contempt which the state court sought to
punish. The former takes the position that Thomas
was jailed as much for uttering the general invitation
as for issuing the specific one. The minority's view is
that he was committed only for the latter act. The
majority's view on this was supported by an argument
that is strained and farfetched. Having accomplished
that much, the case was readily subsumed under accepted principles protecting freedom of speech. The
requirement of registration before one would be permitted to make a public speech to gain support for a
legitimate objective was, accordingly, held to violate
the First Amendment as embodied in the due process
clause of the Fourteenth Amendment. Since Thomas'

67. (1945) 323 U.S. 516.

acts could not be made a crime, neither could they be made the basis for an order whose violation would entail punishment. The minority devoted no part of its opinion to the issue on which the majority decided the case. The minority rejected the claim that the due process clause of the Fourteenth Amendment prohibits a state from requiring paid solicitors for union members to register for purposes of identification. It was dealing with what it held to be essentially a business transaction on behalf of a union which was, with respect to this transaction, a business association.

The case presents a curious situation. It is very likely that the minority would have agreed with the majority's decision had it accepted the latter's interpretation of the case. It is also fairly probable that a majority would have been mustered to support the minority's position on the issue as formulated by it. Such majority might even have included all members of the actual majority in the case. All who participated in the decision of the case may be deemed to have assented to the proposition that a state has the power to regulate labor unions and their activities in the public interest subject to the vague limits defining the area within which freedom of speech is protected. The only regulation thus far held valid prohibited labor unions from denying a person membership by reason of race, color, or creed, and from denying any of its members, by reason thereof, equality of treatment with respect to employment, promotion, and dismissal.[68] This was assailed as violating the due process clause of the Four-

68. Railway Mail Ass'n v. Corsi, (1945) 326 U.S. 88. See also Steele v. L. & N. R.R. Co., (1944) 323 U.S. 192.

teenth Amendment in that it infringed the union's right to select its own membership, and abridged its property rights and freedom of contract. The Court has thus far successfully avoided passing on the validity of numerous regulations of unions imposed by state statute or constitutional provision. The regulations covered such matters as filing reports, prohibiting charges for work permits, and outlawing the closed shop. The principle reason for the Court's refusal has been that the records failed to disclose a case or controversy involving the provisions against which the attack was directed.[69] The basis for this view was that the Court could not know how the state would apply them, and that some applications thereof might be valid. In another instance a case within federal judicial power was admitted to exist, but it was dismissed for want of an authoritative interpretation by the state of the regulation involved in it.[70] The disposition of these cases makes it fairly certain that some of these regulations will be upheld as not violative of due process when an actual case, or one properly presented, requires that a decision be made. It is even more certain that none will be upheld that trench on freedom of speech or press. It may well be that the statement in the majority opinion in *Thomas v. Collins* which mentioned no other limit than that will furnish the major premise for future developments of constitutional law in this field. That the Court will have to face and decide the issues raised by the current trend is certain. It is to be hoped that it will do so with a sense of realism that

69. Ala. State A.F. of L. v. McAdory, (1945) 325 U.S. 450; C.I.O. v. McAdory, (1945) 325 U.S. 472.
70. A.F. of L. v. Watson, (1946) 327 U.S. 582.

makes due allowance for the fact that organized labor is no longer an infant struggling for survival in a society dominated by hostile forces.

The recent strikes in public utilities and other essential industries has created a demand for limiting the right to strike by law, and requiring compulsory arbitration of labor disputes at least in such industries. It was long ago held that the due process clause of the Fourteenth Amendment confers no absolute right to strike. The opinion in that case, *Dorchy v. Kansas*,[71] was written by Justice Brandeis. It sustained the conviction of a union official for calling a strike to compel the employer to pay a former employee a disputed claim for wages. The decision was based on the assumption that the strike was illegal because that was not a permissible purpose justifying the infliction of the injury that the strike would cause the employer to suffer. Justice Brandeis was careful to limit the decision to the specific issue decided. The legislation involved in it was part of the Kansas Court of Industrial Relations Act of 1920. That Act sought to insure continuity of operation in designated industries through a system of compulsory arbitration. This aspect has been before the Supreme Court twice. In the first instance, the Court held invalid the wage provision of an order of the Court of Industrial Relations[72] in such a proceeding. In the second, it invalidated the hours of labor provision of the same order.[73] The employer to whom the order was di-

71. (1924) 264 U.S. 286. Quaere as to the legality of strikes to coerce legislative action?

72. Chas. Wolff Packing Co. v. Court of Industrial Relations of Kansas, (1923) 262 U.S. 522.

73. Chas. Wolff Packing Co. v. Court of Industrial Relations of Kansas,

rected was engaged in the meat-packing business. The wage and hours provisions of the order were dealt with as integral parts of a system of compulsory arbitration. Hence the constitutionality of that system received considerable discussion. The state's attempt to justify it because the packing industry was affected with a public interest was rejected by denying that premise. But not content with that, the Court proceeded to state that compulsory maintenance of continuity of service could be justified only "where the obligation to the public of continuous service is direct, clear and mandatory and arises as a contractual condition express or implied of entering the business either as owner or worker. It can only arise when investment by the owner and entering the employment by the worker create a conventional relation to the public somewhat equivalent to the appointment of officers and the enlistment of soldiers and sailors in the military service." In the opinion in the second of these cases the system was said to infringe "the liberty of contract and rights of property guaranteed by the due process of law clause of the Fourteenth Amendment."

It has been in effect sustained only in *Wilson v. New*[74] in the case of railroads when a threatened strike created a national emergency, and the duration of the relations imposed by the Act of Congress was for a defined and limited period only. The argument by which this legislation was held not violative of the due process clause of the Fifth Amendment is exceedingly obscure. The

---

(1925) 267 U.S. 552. See S. P. Simpson, "Constitutional Limitations on Compulsory Arbitration," 38 Harv. Law Rev. 753 (1925).
74. (1917) 243 U.S. 332.

real basis for sustaining the Adamson Act against all objections was that the dominant national public interest in maintaining railroad transportation justified even this measure which the Court recognized as exceptional.

The question whether compulsory arbitration statutes would today be held invalid is a highly debatable one. If existing authorities were to be followed, they would be held to violate due process if applied to industry generally, and perhaps, in any event if orders made under them were to operate for more than a reasonable cooling-off period. But the current trend has reduced greatly the force of any contentions based on due process clauses. Futhermore, the ultimate basis for sustaining the system in *Wilson v. New* may exist in the case of any major industrial dispute. The threat to the public welfare against which the Adamson Act was aimed may have its source in other industries than those now recognized as public utilities. The coal strikes have proved that. A system of compulsory arbitration would produce that continuity of operations only if the right to strike were also restricted. *Dorchy v. Kansas* has held that due process permits this where the purpose of the strike is illegal. The legislature may define what are illegal purposes, but undoubtedly due process will impose limits on its power to do so. The issue is not whether it could forbid strikes for achieving the many valid objectives of unions merely because continuity of operations would be interrupted thereby. It is whether it may do so as part of a system under which the state or nation itself undertakes to decide finally the issues involved in the dispute. The sacrifices that this will involve for both labor and employer will have to be balanced against the injury to the rest of the community from interruption of production. The Court has recently recognized that it will accept the legislative choice unless that is arbitrary. Should it extend to this problem the broad tolerance of legislative decisions that has marked its decisions sustaining regulations of business, it would undoubtedly hold a compulsory arbitration system not violative of due process as applied to major industries, whether or not they be public businesses or utilities in the ordinary sense of those terms. The denial of the right to strike, so far as reasonably necessary to make the system effective within the range of its validity, would likewise be immune to objections predicated on due process clauses, as would the infliction of punishment for violating a statute or injunction denying such right to strike. It is, however, practically certain that the Thirteenth Amendment would invalidate attempts to impose such punishment upon an individual worker who should refuse of his own accord to continue to work on the terms prescribed in an order made in a compulsory arbitration proceeding. The Court has never decided this, but some of its language in *Pollock v. Williams*[75] fairly implies that it would so construe that Amendment even were the refusal a violation of contract. Justice Jackson in that case affirms that the "undoubted aim of the Thirteenth Amendment as implemented by the Antipeonage Act was not merely to end slavery but to maintain a system of completely free and voluntary labor throughout the United States." While he recognizes exceptions, all his examples involved

75. (1944) 322 U.S. 4.

compulsory labor for the government. His language, though dictum, probably forms the basic premise from which the prohibitions of the Thirteenth Amendment would be derived. There is a distinction between a single individual's exercise of his right to quit work and his quitting as part of concerted action with other employees to defeat a valid governmental policy. No federal constitutional provision prohibits government from using the full complement of pressure devices at its disposal to that end. The system of compulsory arbitration of labor disputes may not solve the problem of protecting the public interest threatened by such controversies, but it would probably be upheld today in some areas of economic activity, and within the limits indicated above, as not violating any constitutional rights of either the employer or the employee.

The protection of contractual rights is essential to economic planning in a private enterprise economy. Such a system requires an intricate maze of future commitments on whose fulfillment the entrepreneur must in general be able to rely in planning his activities. General insecurity with respect to these matters tends in the long run to higher prices, and, if it becomes sufficiently serious, to hamper the nation's production. Not only must the entreprenuer be able to count on performance by others of the promises made to him, he must also have some assurance that the monetary unit that measures the value of those promises possesses considerable stability and be not made an object of governmental manipulation. The depression that began in 1929 and continued in some measure into 1940 produced a great deal of legislation seriously affecting the security of established contractual relations. The state moratory laws aimed to relieve a particular class of debtors, the First and Second Frazier-Lemke Acts sought to protect the same group, and the federal legislation dealing with the monetary system had as one of its objectives the relief of debtors generally by raising the price level. The principal objection to the state laws was that they impaired the obligation of contracts in violation of Article I, Section 10, of the federal Constitution. The due process clause of the Fifth Amendment thereto was one of the major obstacles to the federal legislation just referred to.

The leading case passing on the validity of state moratory legislation is *Home Building & Loan Association v. Blaisdell*.[76] The state statute involved provided for a judicial proceeding by the mortgagor for extending the period of redemption for such period as the court might deem just. The extension could be granted only on condition that the mortgagor pay all, or a reasonable part of the income from, or rental value of, the mortgaged property, to be applied to the payment of taxes, insurance, interest, and mortgage indebtedness as the court might determine. Provision was made for terminating the extension if the mortgagor defaulted in these matters, and it was to end in any event on May 1, 1935, a date approximately two years after the date of the enactment of the statute. The property involved in the case had already been sold by the mortgagee for default on the part of the mortgagor when the statute was enacted, but the redemption period had not yet expired then. The statute was held not to impair the

76. (1934) 290 U.S. 398.

obligation of contracts as applied to a case of this kind. The importance of the decision lies in the broad principles invoked to sustain the law. The state was said to have authority to "safeguard the vital interests of its people" though this involves modifying or abrogating existing contracts. The majority opinion invokes the growing recognition of public needs as a reason for preventing "the perversion of the (contract) clause" into "an instrument to throttle the capacity of the States to protect their fundamental interests." The theory that there is implied in every contract a term reserving to the states their sovereign powers to protect those interests is not only expressed but applied. The factors that made the decision fairly easy were the existence of an emergency, the limited period during which the remedy was postponed, and that the conditions of the right to postponement protected the mortgagee's interest in a reasonable manner. It was a 5 to 4 decision. The minority based itself on prior decisions which certainly lent more support to its position than to that of the majority. In a recent decision the Court showed itself quite disinclined to question the legislative judgment that conditions warranted an extension of the policy by a statute enacted in 1943, a new emergency being invoked to furnish the basis therefor.[77]

At a time when mortgagees were frequently the only bidders at a foreclosure sale, legislation was enacted to prevent them from profiting thereby at the expense of the debtor. These laws limited the right to obtain a deficiency judgment if the value of the mortgaged property at the time of the sale was at least equal to the

77. East New York Savings Bank v. Hahn, (1945) 326 U.S. 230.

debt secured thereby. In view of the long-standing power of courts of equity to protect the debtors' interest in a somewhat similar manner by their refusal to confirm a sale at a grossly inadequate price, such legislation was readily sustained even as applied to pre-existing mortgages.[78] Federal legislation for the protection of farm debtors was first held to deprive creditors of their property without due process of law because it failed adequately to protect their interests.[79] It was sustained after amendments had remedied this failure.[80] In none of the cases decided since 1933 did the Court sustain the application to pre-existing contracts of legislation that failed to give the creditors' interests reasonable protection. On the contrary it held such laws violative of the contract, or due process clauses, or both. State moratory laws frequently did for large groups of ordinary mortgage debtors something comparable to what equity receiverships accomplished for embarrassed corporate debtors. The public interest protected was not the same, but often was at least as important. Depressions have always been the occasion for such legislation. They are times when losses have finally to be recognized and realized. So long as legislation does not shift the losses to the creditor permanently and in such a manner as to force him in effect to furnish the debtor with capital for the old or new ventures, moratory legislation is not likely seriously to

78. Richmond Mtge & Loan Corp. v. Wachovia Bank & Trust Co., (1937) 300 U.S. 124. See also Honeyman v. Jacobs, (1939) 306 U.S. 539, and Honeyman v. Hanan, (1937) 302 U.S. 375.

79. Louisville Joint Stock Land Bank v. Radford, (1935) 295 U.S. 555.

80. Wright v. Vinton Branch of Mountain Trust Bank of Roanoke, (1937) 300 U.S. 440.

affect the maintenance of a private enterprise economy. While the legislation induced by the depression of 1929-1940 would undoubtedly have been held invalid prior to 1933, the Court did not depart from earlier precedents as widely as in its post-1933 revisions of some other provisions of the Constitution.

The manipulation of the national currency to effect the temporary redistribution of income and wealth presents a more serious threat to the stability of any economic system, and hence to that of a private enterprise economy. The federal government is in a strategic position to do this. It can exercise its power to borrow in such a way as to monetize the national debt either by issuing paper money or through its control of the banking system. A considerable part of the debt incurred to finance the late war was monetized in the latter manner. But it has available another power for manipulating the currency, that of adjusting its monetary standard. This was an important element in the New Deal's policy, and was given the attractive and seductive name of reflation. For more than a generation preceding 1933 farsighted investors had sought to guard themselves against this risk by requiring so-called "gold clauses" of one sort or another to be inserted in the bonds they purchased. The result was that these clauses were found not only in the bonds of private issuers but in those of the United States as well. In order to insure that the government's devaluation policy accomplish its objective, Congress invalidated such clauses in both previously and subsequently issued bonds. This provision was unsuccessfully assailed as violating the due process clause of the Fifth Amendment in the case of private bonds.[81] The substance of the Court's argument was that the Constitution was designed to provide a uniform currency throughout the United States, and that all contracts must be deemed to have been made subject to be defeated or impaired through an exercise by Congress of its power to coin money. Since private contracts can neither restrict nor defeat that power, it included that of directly declaring all such contracts invalid, whether entered into before or after such legislation. The gold clauses were stated to interfere with a valid federal policy, or, at least, Congress could not be said to have acted arbitrarily when it decided that they did so. It was accordingly held that such legislation was within the power of Congress and did not violate the due process clause of the Fifth Amendment. The majority invoked the fact that debtors who receive their income in devalued dollars would be required to pay their debts in terms of the old dollar were this legislation held invalid. There is force to the minority's contention that the purpose of the Act was not to remove an obstacle to a uniform currency but to destroy certain valuable contract rights. The argument that gold clauses interfered with achieving a uniform currency is specious. The currency was no less uniform before the Act than after it.

The holders of United States bonds containing a gold clause scored a nominal victory.[82] The provision of Section 4 of the Fourteenth Amendment: "The validity of the public debt of the United States, authorized by law, . . . shall not be questioned," as well as the assertion of

81. Norman v. Balt. & Ohio R. Co., (1935) 294. U.S 240.
82. Perry v. United States, (1935) 294 U.S. 330.

a lack of power in Congress to repudiate the government debt, was held to void the application of the Gold Clause Act to federal bonds containing the gold clause. But an impossible requirement was imposed for establishing proof of loss. It is not of record that any such bondholder has ever benefited from the ruling in his favor in *Perry v. United States.*

The decisions in these cases deprived prior investors in bonds and other long-term contracts of valuable rights. They have established principles that would render valueless any such provision in future transactions were the Gold Clause Act to be repealed. For practical purposes investors have been deprived of a reliable method for guarding themselves against inflation. These decisions, and those dealing with the validity of state moratory legislation, have reduced the constitutional protection of contractual rights. Whether they have in actuality reduced the motive to accumulate capital can probably not be definitely determined. The situation has contained too many other factors to justify any conclusion on the matter. What is significant is that they are in line with the general trend towards giving legislative bodies an increasing power over capital and the regulation of business generally. This is but one aspect of the expansion of government that has been so much accelerated in the United States since 1933.

It is a fair interpretation of the decisions rendered since 1933 that the scope of the due process clauses of the federal Constitution has been both expanded and contracted. They no longer afford the interests of property and business the protection they once did. On the other hand, the interests of labor are receiving greater protection, particularly those of its activities that may be viewed as exercises of the workers' personal liberty. This explains the decisions holding picketing to be a form of free speech or press, although it is undeniable that its effectiveness in an industrial dispute is frequently, if not generally, due to something other than the persuasive force of communicating ideas as to the issues involved in the controversy. The Court has accepted the position of Justice Brandeis, stated in his concurring opinion in the *St. Joseph Stock Yards Case*,[83] that the due process clauses protect personal liberty more extensively than rights of property. It has also been intimated by the Court that the presumption of constitutionality may have a "narrower scope" of operation "when legislation appears on its face to be within a specific prohibition of the Constitution, such as those of the first ten amendments" than when applied to that "affecting ordinary commercial transactions."[84] Justice Stone expressly included in his statement rights of the character of those protected by the first ten Amendments so far as they are "embraced within the Fourteenth." Since 1933 the decisions have definitely reflected this shift of emphasis. The *Gold Clause Cases* are in line with that trend, as are the decisions involving the moratory legislation of the depression period. All lay a firm basis for a more intensive federal and state regulation of the nation's economic activities, especially those of business. It remains to be seen whether the activities of labor, which are also clearly

83. (1936) 298 U.S. 38.

84. United States v. Carolene Products Co., (1938) 304 U.S. 144, footnote 4 to Justice Stone's opinion.

of an economic nature, will receive a greater amount of protection through judicial construction of existing federal constitutional limitations.

V

Some Implications of Recent Trends

The three preceding Chapters have presented a survey of current developments in an important area of our constitutional law. It was shown that since 1933 the Supreme Court has so construed the Constitution as to sustain a great expansion of federal powers, a relaxation of important limitations on state powers, an acceptance of a more extensive and intensive regulation of business, and an increase in the protection of personal liberty in areas other than business. It is extremely unlikely that there will be any general retreat from these positions within any period now foreseeable. The real question is how much further these trends are likely to be carried. It is obvious that the answer will depend on many factors, some of which are already present. These include certain political, social, and economic philosophies that gained wide adherence during the depression and are even today accepted tenets of popular thought. The dogma that government should assume an important and permanent role in achieving economic stability and a more just social order is not likely to be discarded. Impatience with its practice during the recent war may weaken it temporarily, but it is certain to revive on the first appearance of economic difficulties. The economic theories, on which much of the New Deal legislation was based, are still accepted by influential groups as offering the only road to our salvation. That the New Deal merely tapped the resources available to government to regulate the national economy was demonstrated by our war experience. It is difficult to determine how far the precedents from that period could be used to sustain similar government peacetime controls. It will be safest to ignore them, and limit the discussion to the emergency and reform measures enacted after 1933 that had no direct connection with war or the preparation therefor.

The dominant idea in today's political and economic thought is the need for governmental economic planning if our resources and labor are to yield the maximum social welfare and economic stability. The system in which the separate plannings of a vast number of individual planners were integrated through competitive markets is assumed to have been proved inadequate for organizing the nation's and the world's economic resources and activities. It is not necessary for our purposes to appraise the soundness of this assumption. It is sufficient that it exists, is likely to continue to exist, and is certain to influence governmental action. The most extreme form of government planning is that in which government itself assumes the functions of entrepreneur and capitalist. Such a system of state capitalism is not an immediate prospect in this nation. Some expansion of public ownership and operation of business enterprises is quite probable. It is doubtful that it will be such as to make our economy predominantly one of state capitalism. The Constitution interposes few, if any, barriers to even the general adoption of that system.[1] However, the regulation of private enterprise, including labor, is likely for long to remain our principal method of government economic planning. Since the major part of our economic activities involve interstate commerce at some stage, and since many of the obstacles to the national welfare are rooted in causes operating throughout the nation, the federal government is bound to play a larger role than the states in any planning program that may be undertaken. Its activities will accordingly receive the emphasis which their greater importance merits.

The methods of control adopted will be in large part determined by views as to what are the evils to be remedied and their causes. The two principal inadequacies charged against what is called the unplanned competitive economy have been its instability and its failure to provide a socially desirable distribution of the national income. It is asserted that the recurrent cycle of "boom and bust" is an inherent and inevitable characteristic of that system. Each entrepreneur's pursuit of profits, guided by his own estimates of the supply and demand for his product on the basis of his own interpretation of its market price, is claimed inevitably to result in its overproduction. The facts adduced to sup-

1. It has been stated that a state may engage in any business, now generally conducted by private enterprise, if the legislature considers it for the general public good to engage therein; Chas. Wolff Packing Co. v. Court of Industrial Relations of Kansas, (1923) 262 U.S. 522. See also Green v. Frazier, (1920) 253 U.S. 233. The distribution of power between the federal government and the states made by the Constitution might limit the area of economic activity within which the federal government could assume the functions of owner and entrepreneur. The recent expansion of federal powers has, however, considerably reduced the size of this area.

port this generally show merely that the production of goods and services has failed to maintain that balance between production of the various goods and services which must exist if continuity of production is to be maintained for all of them. This is due in practically every instance to the price structure and the price-cost relationship. However, the remedy that has usually been proposed has been to bolster demand by increasing the purchasing power of certain groups so that they may translate their wants into effective demand. Another factor stressed in the theory advanced to support this latter type of approach is that the imbalance between production and the effective demand for goods and services is due to saving in excess of the immediate demand for capital. The failure to adjust production to this factor must be compensated for by pumping purchasing power to those who can thus furnish the effective demand lost through the savings that might otherwise have furnished it. This shifting of purchasing power may be accomplished either through price control or outright subsidies. This is the substance of the theory as to how economic stability is to be secured, or at least as to the method for reducing the instability of the present system. It is in part relevant also to the objective of establishing a more desirable social order through the redistribution of the national wealth and income. It is, however, but one approach to that problem. Another is to permit an initial distribution without direct intervention in the economic processes of production and distribution, and then to modify the result by a redistribution through the use of the government's powers to tax and borrow. This is an ancient form of accomplishing the result desired, and, while not without important consequences for a private enterprise economy, is, on the whole, less of an immediate disturbing factor to it. The federal government and the states have both resorted to regulation and taxation to redistribute wealth and income.

This analysis suggests the vital points at which government will have to intervene in directing and controlling the nation's economy to achieve what are generally accepted as its objectives. It was no accident that the federal government sought to limit the production of many agricultural products. There are at present four methods available for so doing, none of which is a regulation of production in a constitutional sense. The method held invalid in *United States v. Butler*[2] is now valid. It is an expensive method since its use involves the subsidization of those who cooperate with the government in carrying out its policy. It also has the disadvantage, from the government's point of view, of being voluntary. It is unlikely to be widely used except when the main purpose is the distribution of subsidies. Another method is that of price control. This is available if the product is marketed in the interstate market. It has been held that the federal government may regulate the prices of coal and of milk under such circumstances. The reasons sustaining this apply to any commodity. But price control indirectly affects either the supply or demand, and particular kinds of price control will tend to restrict production. The levy of certain kinds of taxes on the interstate shipment offers a convenient device for accomplishing the same result. But the

2. (1936) 297 U.S. 1.

method that has been found most effective is the fixing of quotas for the interstate marketing of commodities. Since rational men producing for a given market are not likely in the long run to continue to produce an excess over their quota, the result in fact is production control whatever it may be for purposes of bringing it within the federal commerce power. It has thus far been used almost wholly in connection with agricultural commodities. The reasoning by which it was sustained makes it equally applicable to other commodities, to manufactured articles as well as to raw materials.

The quota laws were not in form a prohibition of interstate commerce since the producer could market the excess upon payment of what was in fact a prohibitive tax or penalty. Subsequent to the first decision sustaining them, the Court decided the *Darby Case*.[3] In it the commerce power was construed to confer upon Congress an absolute discretion to prohibit completely the interstate transportation of goods. The only limit on its power is the due process clause of the Fifth Amendment. In no decision has this been held violated by any prohibition thus far passed upon. The same case gave an extreme turn to the principle that Congress may do anything necessary and proper to carrying its commerce power into execution. It held that it could directly regulate the conditions of employment in aid of its policy to deny the channels of interstate commerce to goods produced under substandard employment conditions as defined by it. This raises some interesting possibilities as to how far production may be limited by the marketing quota system. If the Court meant what

3. United States v. Darby, (1941) 312 U.S. 100.

it said when stating that Congress is free to adopt any policy it wishes in the field of interstate commerce, then the commerce clause interposes no obstacle to federal legislation requiring that commodities produced in a given area be marketed in some other given market area. This could be used to build up the industries of one section of the country at the expense of competitors in other sections. It might even be used to give each state the equivalent of a protective tariff. It is unlikely that Congress will ever enact such absurdities into law, but the possibility exists so far as the commerce clause is concerned. The only protection afforded producers for the interstate market from such legislation is the due process clause of the Fifth Amendment. If it could so stifle producers, it could equally prohibit buying from producers whose goods had been excluded from the area within which the purchase was made. The purchaser's only protection would be the same due process clause. Both producer and purchaser might object not only that it was an unreasonable interference with their economic freedom but also that it denied them the equal protection of the law. While the Court has never yet held any classification made by Congress invalid on that score, it has never stated that the arbitrary regulation which due process prohibits does not include unreasonable discrimination. However, the recent trend is to deny economic interests, other than those of labor, any protection whatever under the due process clauses. There is at least some likelihood that the Court might consider the suggested measures to be beyond their elastic limits.

The most extreme extension of federal commerce

power yet made occurred in *Wickard v. Filburn*[4] which sustained the inclusion of wheat fed to his livestock and that used to produce flour for family use in the producer's marketing quota. The implications of this become rather alarming when joined with those that can be based on one of the arguments used to uphold that definition. It was stated that Congress could fix prices for wheat shipped in interstate commerce, and that, therefore, it could remove the competition of homegrown wheat to protect its price policy with respect to wheat produced for the interstate market. This competition would of course operate whether or not the competitor was also producing for that market. Hence the commerce power would permit legislation prohibiting any person from producing wheat for home consumption. But the government's price policy for wheat might be thwarted by the production of substitutes for wheat for home use. If this too may be prohibited, a fortiori would the production of wheat and wheat substitutes for distribution in the intrastate market. After all, this would merely be applying to this problem a principle already sustained with respect to federal price control of milk. The principles developed in the wheat quota cases would be equally applicable to other commodities moving in interstate commerce. Nor has their application been made to depend upon any factor that would restrict these control devices to commodities comprising a significant factor in interstate trade. Again, the due process clause is the individual's only protection against such measures. It was invoked by the farmer in *Wickard v. Filburn*, but rather summarily rejected. One

4. (1942) 317 U.S. 111.

reason therefor was the existence of other methods for dealing with his excess wheat than selling it on payment of a penalty. The other was that "It is hardly lack of due process for the Government to regulate that which it subsidizes." It is certain that this basis for denying that a regulation violates due process will not be extended to one that restricts liberty of the person. The federal government has acquired a growing habit of granting subsidies. Does this argument imply that their recipients lose their privilege of invoking due process against any regulation of their economic activities which Congress may wish to impose? Or is it limited to regulations affecting those economic activities in connection with which the subsidy is granted? Probably the latter. That was the situation in *Wickard v. Filburn*. Even so limited, it may prove a wholesome deterrent to subsidy seekers.

The *Darby Case* sustained a direct regulation of the production of goods for the interstate market as a proper means for realizing a policy which Congress was free to fix for interstate commerce. The quota system is an indirect method for promoting Congressional policy in the same field. There would now seem to be no obstacle to limiting production for the interstate market directly, and likewise production for the intrastate market. Nor is there any logical basis against using that method to prevent the competition of substitute commodities. Neither the commerce nor due process clauses would interpose any obstacle not equally applicable to the indirect method of establishing marketing quotas. But this part of the theory espoused in the *Darby Case* has important implications for another problem closely related to production control however implemented. This is the problem of directing or controlling investment. The very existence of production control will tend to deter the entrance of new capital into the controlled fields as long as existing capacity is adequate to produce the quotas fixed by the government. But government may choose not to rely upon this automatic response to its policy, and deem it necessary to resort to compulsory controls to prevent adventurers from complicating its problem. One way to secure this would be to deny newcomers a quota or impose conditions on their right to receive one. Another would be to permit new or additional investment in the fields for which production control has been established only on compliance with specified conditions, or to prohibit it unconditionally. None of these would be any less substantially related to interstate commerce than the regulations sustained in the *Darby Case*. Their validity under the commerce clause may be taken for granted.

The due process clause poses a more difficult issue. To deny a person a quota, or impose conditions on his right to one, is a serious impairment of his economic freedom. This is equally true of the suggested controls of investment. That they are integral parts of a plan for attaining a valid federal policy in the field of interstate commerce is in their favor. That they tend to give a particular group of producers some of the advantages of a monopoly is a factor militating against their validity that would have been given more weight a quarter of a century ago than it is now likely to receive. The Court has sustained legislation permitting monopolistic business practices through private agreement under the guise of prohibiting unfair methods of competition.[5] The principles on which *New State Ice Company v. Liebmann*[6] was decided would render these methods invalid. But it is extremely doubtful that this case is still law although it has never been expressly overruled. Even the majority of the Court in it recognized that such controls would be valid in the case of businesses affected with a public interest. The *Nebbia Case*[7] has expanded that concept to include practically every business. This alone might suffice to sustain the validity of the suggested control devices. Furthermore the dissenting opinion of Justice Brandeis in the *New State Ice Company Case* represents current ideas on this problem more nearly than does its prevailing opinion. The likelihood is very great that the Court today would sustain against due process objections every one of the control devices described above.

Considerations of the same general character would also sustain other methods against attacks based on the commerce and due process clauses. These include prohibiting the interstate shipment of the products of new plants, or requiring all businesses engaged in interstate commerce to be licensed by the federal government and attaching appropriate conditions to the grant of licenses. The decisions sustaining certain provisions of the Federal Power Act and the Holding Company Act[8] indicate the vast possibilities of the latter method. The

5. Old Dearborn Distributing Co. v. Seagram Distillers Corp., (1936) 299 U.S. 183.

6. (1932) 285 U.S. 262.

7. Nebbia v. New York, (1934) 291 U.S. 502.

8. North American Co. v. Securities and Exchange Commission, (1946) 327 U.S. 686; American Lt. & Pr. Co. v. Securities and Exchange Commission, (1946) 329 U.S. 90.

power to tax could also be used. Taxes on the undistributed profits of businesses whose expansion was to be limited or prevented could effectively close one source of funds required to finance expansion. A discriminatory tax against new outside investments in such businesses would probably not be necessary, but would nevertheless be available. Each of these methods involves a use of the power to classify in exercising the taxing power. That a tax classification is being used in aid of a social or economic policy is often made the basis for holding it to be not violative of the equal protection clause of the Fourteenth Amendment. The same principle applies in determining whether a classification made in connection with a federal tax is reasonable and therefore not violative of the due process clause of the Fifth Amendment. Since the suggested classifications are used to support a national economic policy that Congress may promote, they would undoubtedly be sustained. Neither can we ignore the federal government's power over investment banking in dealing with this general question. The conclusion is warranted that it has available several instruments for effectively influencing and controlling the direction of investment in support of any national economic policy that it may validly adopt. The decisions defining the scope of its commerce power and the extent to which it may use its powers to tax and spend for the national general welfare afford it a wide range for the selection of such policies. Similar methods could also be employed to secure such allocation of raw materials as would be required.

A great deal of federal regulatory and prohibitory legislation has been based upon the national government's control over interstate transportation. Interstate commerce also includes interstate commercial transactions. Their consummation generally contemplates interstate movement of some kind. The power of Congress directly to regulate such transactions is as broad as its power to regulate interstate movements. The Sherman Anti-Trust and the Federal Trade Commission Acts are primarily concerned with this phase of interstate commerce. The Codes promulgated under authority of the National Industrial Recovery Act were also concerned therewith. Congressional price control legislation is a conspicuous example of a recent extension in this field of interstate commerce. It had prevailed in interstate transportation for a long period prior to its adoption for interstate sales. This represented an important change in policy because of the functions prices perform in a private enterprise economy. They constitute its principal regulatory mechanism, and thus a major factor in its system of planning. They not only guide producers in arriving at the decisions that have to be made in any system, but also serve to allocate the national income among those participating in the production and distribution of goods and services. Government price fixing is thus an interference with the planning mechanism of such an economy and a method for redistributing income. It is in the former of these aspects that it will now be considered. Since it is generally accepted that the intervention touches one of the most vital points of the existing system, it is important to determine how far the federal government may resort to it in industries other than public utilities as these are generally defined.

The extent of its power is first of all a matter of the scope of its commerce power. The reasons for sustaining it with respect to milk and coal are equally applicable to other commodities. It may fix prices for interstate sales by the producer to the distributor, by any distributor to another, and by the last of them to the local retailer. It may also fix the price for any retail sale in interstate commerce. It has already been decided that it may fix prices on intrastate sales at least so far as appropriate to protect its interstate price policy. This was held in a case in which the intrastate sales were made in competition with the regulated interstate sales.[9] It may fairly be asked whether it could control the prices of the local retail sales of goods whose interstate sale prices it has undertaken to fix. There is no doubt that this might be necessary to realizing the objectives aimed at by its regulation of interstate sales. It is certain that this would be held an adequate basis for bringing the control of such retail sale prices within the commerce power. Similar considerations would justify federal price fixing of locally produced competitive commodities, and of competitive substitutes whether or not locally produced. Since the expansion of federal powers on the basis of the commerce clause reflects a keen appreciation of the organic character of our national economic system, the Court might well hold that Congress could regulate also those prices that are production costs of the commodity whose interstate sales have been taken under its protection. This is especially so where the prices fixed for such sales are minimum prices intended to protect the incomes of their producers. Since

9. United States v. Wrightwood Dairy Co., (1942) 315 U.S. 110.

prices constitute a rather complex and closely integrated system, it may well be that the commerce clause may be the key to an expansive system of federal price-fixing at every level. While the recent cases have involved minimum prices, the principles would be equally applicable to maximum prices. The objective would be different, but still legitimate. What was asserted as to the possibilities of federal price control is, therefore, true whatever form it may assume.

The difficulties experienced during the war with general federal price control may deter experimenting with it in peace time. There was a long period when the due process clause of the Fourteenth Amendment restricted state price control within fairly narrow limits. During that same period federal price regulation would have been similarly limited by the due process clause of the Fifth Amendment. The *District of Columbia Rent Law Case*[10] is conclusive proof of that. The limits once derived from the due process clauses have now been practically eliminated by the principles on which the *Nebbia Case* was decided. This involved minimum prices, but it would be impossible to restrict the effects of those principles to that form of price regulation. The circumstances that may be invoked to justify price-fixing will vary according as minimum or maximum prices are being fixed, but this is likely hereafter to affect only the specific reasoning by which the system will be sustained. Both forms involve a distribution of income differing from that which would have occurred but for the government's intervention. This is somewhat more obvious where the prices fixed are minima, but is

10. Block v. Hirsh, (1921) 256 U.S. 135.

equally true where they are maxima. Prices fixed by government can still function to guide producers of the regulated commodities or services. They lose some of their regulatory importance because they distort the price relationships to which the distribution of labor, materials and capital plant have been adjusted. But the Constitution today permits it within areas of economic activity formerly closed to it.

The changes effected in the relations of labor and capital by legislation enacted after 1933 by both the federal government and the states is, perhaps, the most important development of recent times. The barriers which the due process clauses once interposed to legislation protecting unions in their efforts to organize the workers from hostile interference by employers have been completely eliminated. Legislation compelling employers to bargain collectively with the chosen representatives of their employees has been enacted by both the federal government and some states. The former has done so over a wide range of business and industry on the basis of the commerce clause. The question is whether, and, if so, how far, it can extend this policy and labor's right to organize beyond the limits set by present legislation. The theory on which such legislation has been sustained is that labor disputes resulting from the denial of these rights may cause strikes that burden interstate commerce. Attempts to limit this power to industries deriving their raw materials from other states or selling their products in interstate commerce, or both, have proved unsuccessful. The National Labor Relations Act has been held applicable to an employer not engaged in interstate commerce,[11] and to apply to an employer producing electric power sold to railroads for use in moving interstate trains.[12] It is quite immaterial whether the threat to interstate commerce originates in interstate or local commerce. The local retail merchant who sells goods produced in other states could validly be subjected to the same kind of regulation. A strike of his employees would affect interstate commerce injuriously by reducing the market of the out-of-state producer. There is no constitutional reason for not extending the scope of the regulations provided for by the National Labor Relations Act to every employee in any way connected with the production and every stage in the distribution of goods that move in interstate commerce during any part of this process. This is equally true with respect to the regulation of wages and hours of such employees. The legislation since 1933 has been uniformly favorable to labor, at least that part of it that either was already organized or succeeded in organizing with the aid of such legislation and its administration. The manner in which organized labor used its newly won powers provoked a reaction that has already led to important restrictive state legislation and appears likely to result in similar action by Congress. There is no requirement in the commerce clause that limits its exercise to legislation advantageous to labor. Interstate commerce may suffer from its activities as well as from those of business. That has already received judicial recognition. Congress may reasonably believe that monopolistic practices by organized labor are as grave

11. N.L.R.B. v. Fainblatt, (1939) 306 U.S. 601.
12. Consolidated Edison Co. v. N.L.R.B., (1938) 305 U.S. 197.

a threat to such commerce as are those of industry. It is inconceivable that the Court today would go back on the *Darby Case* and hold that the prohibition of a closed shop within the range of employment covered by the National Labor Relations and the Fair Labor Standards Acts was not within the commerce power of Congress. The same thing would apply to other union security devices as well. None of the measures that have been suggested in Congress are outside its commerce power if limited to employees and employers who either now are or could be covered by those Acts under principles that the present Court has announced and applied time and again. The Congressional power to regulate labor relations in or affecting interstate commerce will expand or contract with the expansion or contraction of the scope of the commerce clause in other fields.

The only possibility that any such legislation might be held invalid is that it be found to violate the due process clause of the Fifth Amendment or the Thirteenth Amendment. The latter would be relevant if legislation should attempt to compel a person to continue in his employment against his will or exert such unreasonable legal pressure upon him as would lead him to prefer that to the alternatives which the legislation offered him. The prohibition of strikes would probably be held not to involve any violation of this amendment. That was discussed when dealing with the validity of compulsory arbitration. The main obstacle to all the proposed legislation is the due process clause. The organization of a union involves an exercise of the right of association which the due process clause protects, but only within rather vaguely defined limits. No court would hold due process violated by legislation prohibiting such organizations as the Ku Klux Klan. Every court would find it violated by a statute prohibiting the organization of an American Legion Post. The right to organize a labor union to promote the economic interests of its members is just as much protected as that of organizing a Legion Post. However much due process may protect the right of association, it does not immunize the organization that results from its exercise against reasonable regulation of its internal affairs and its relations with nonmembers. In defining the permissible extent of legislative control over the conduct of labor unions a basic consideration is that their principal functions are economic as much as are those of investors who combine their capital to prosecute a business enterprise. There is no doubt that many of their practices which are now the target of proposed legislation involve advantages to both them and the employers with whom they bargain. This is true of industry-wide collective bargaining and the closed shop and other forms of union security. But due process does not prevent interference with practices merely because they give advantage to the parties immediately involved. It does not even prevent the regulation of practices that in some respects benefit the general public. The same practices may injure other interests which the legislature may reasonably rate more important than those that benefit therefrom. It is unlikely that the Court which has shown itself eager to defer to the legislature's choice of competing interests would hold an Act of Congress limiting or even prohibiting industry-wide collective bargaining violative of the due process clause of the Fifth Amendment.

The closed shop issue merits separate consideration. It is monopolistic in character even when supplemented by the permit-card system. The Supreme Court has recognized that the choice of economic policies to be promoted lies with the legislature. Its virtual overruling of *New State Ice Company v. Liebmann* expands the area within which it would tolerate legislative regulations conferring some degree of monopolistic privileges. In the absence of legislation or common law rule prohibiting it, a union and an employer are free to enter into a closed shop arrangement. No nonmember would have any legally recognized interest injured thereby however much his economic interests might be affected. A statute that did no more than give legislative sanction to this situation would clearly not violate due process. The question is whether the legislature may go beyond this either by establishing the closed shop or by prohibiting it. Either of these would nominally restrict the freedom of contract of both the union and the employer. The former, however, would in fact put the force of government back of a policy which most unions desire to enforce, but would be a significant impairment of the usual employer's economic freedom. The prohibition of the closed shop would reverse these positions. So far as they only are considered, it is merely a question whether the due process clause protects the economic interests of the one more fully than those of the other. Its language contains no suggestion of a preference between them. But these are not the only interests involved. A statute imposing the closed shop subjects the economic

interests of workers who are not union members to control by a private group possessing some degree of monopolistic power over employment opportunities. A statute prohibiting the closed shop would protect nonmembers against this form of economic compulsion. The
employer's freedom of speech has been held not to
include the right to use speech under circumstances
that transform it into an exertion of economic power.
The protection of labor against the employer's use
of his superior economic power is not prohibited by
the due process clause. If the legislature may protect
labor against the employer's use of his economic
power, equally may it protect one group of labor
against the economic power of another group of labor.
It is a well-established principle that due process does
not invalidate legislation aimed at monopoly and
monopolistic practices. The likelihood is that a statute
prohibiting a closed shop would be sustained. The case
is not quite as clear with respect to legislation imposing
the closed shop. The incidence of such policy upon the
interests of the groups affected has already been described. The injury to nonmembers of a union might
bring a decision invalidating such legislation. It is probably the only interest that would cause the Court to
reject the legislative choice. It might be rated so highly
as to induce the Court to hold the legislation arbitrary.
But the result is far from certain. The considerations
bearing on the validity of legislation concerning the
closed shop would apply to some extent, but not as fully,
to statutes dealing with other union security devices.

There are certain measures that the legislature might
consider desirable so far as the closed shop is permitted

or imposed. These are indicated by the monopolistic character of the closed shop. The right to it might be conditioned upon compliance with certain terms prescribed by the legislature. These might include requiring a union to admit qualified persons on reasonable terms, and regulating the initiation fees and union dues. The former would adequately protect nonmembers if administered by public authority. No court would deny the legislature power to protect their interests. That the means suggested would be reasonable few would deny. Its selection lies well within the area of legislative discretion as judicially defined. The regulation of union fees and dues is merely another instance of price control. There is nothing sacrosanct about these particular prices excluding them from the principles of the *Nebbia Case.* In fact, to the extent that the closed shop is monopolistic, the regulation of these prices could be justified under principles accepted even before that case was decided. The probabilities are greatly in favor of the view that the suggested legislation would be held not to violate due process clauses.

The other major change in employer-employee relations concerns minimum wage legislation. The area within which the commerce clause permits Congress to regulate prices has already been indicated. Wages are a price. Hence what was said on that matter with respect to other prices can be applied to wages. The validity of minimum wages under due process clauses has been definitively established. The question is whether Congress or the states may also fix maximum wages. There is nothing in the commerce clause to prevent Congress from so doing. The only important issue arises under the due process clause of the Fifth Amendment in the case of federal action, and of the Fourteenth Amendment for state action. That the mere fact that legislative prices are maximum prices does not render them obnoxious to due process clauses is so firmly established as to require no citation of authorities. The first case holding government price-fixing consistent with the due process clause of the Fourteenth Amendment involved maximum prices. The due process clauses mention neither prices nor wages. They refer to liberty and property. The interest denoted by prices and wages is an economic one. There are distinctions between wages and other prices, but either may be the cause for so retarding the functioning of the national economy as to affect the general interest adversely. Both may be regulated to prevent that. If the source of the obstacle to the public welfare is an economic maladjustment with respect to prices, due process does not prevent its correction by price regulation. The Court explicitly recognized this in the *Nebbia Case*. No one conversant with economic matters would deny that high wage rates can retard production as effectively as high material prices, and more so than high utility rates for ultimate consumers. A legislative judgment that such a situation existed in a particular area of economic activity would scarcely be set aside by any court today. They have accepted legislative judgments supported by some rather tenuous evidence. The due process clauses interpose no absolute barrier to the legislative fixing of maximum wages. The circumstances that would make it reasonable differ from those justifying minimum wage laws. That they may exist is certain. No occasion has yet arisen for determining whether there is a limit below which such maxima might not validly be fixed. It is reasonable to expect that one will be discovered in the due process clauses analagous to the prohibition against confiscatory public utility rates. However, the necessity for such a limit in the case of rent-fixing during the war has been denied so far as any particular landlord was concerned. Among the reasons urged to support that view was the legal privilege of the landlord to decline to rent his premises. The legal right of a worker to refuse employment at the fixed maximum might thus defeat his claim that due process imposed a lower limit on a legislatively fixed maximum wage. This would be as unrealistic in his case as in that of the landlord. Yet the precedent exists, but it need not be followed.

It is recognized almost universally that the control of the national economy will have to be done by the federal government. The states can only cooperate or supplement it within areas permitted by Congress. The discussion thus far has therefore stressed federal action. One further method available to the national government should be mentioned. The commerce clause permits it to require those wishing to engage in interstate commerce to procure a license. The decisions sustaining the Federal Power Act and the Public Utility Holding Company Act enable Congress to attach conditions to the grant of such license. A vast system of regulation can thus be created. That Congress could require federal incorporation of all corporations wishing to engage in interstate commerce is certain. Nor would the commerce clause prevent it from limiting the right to engage in such commerce to corporations so organized, excluding individuals therefrom. The due process clause of the Fourteenth Amendment has been held not violated by closing the banking field to individuals. But even today it would probably be held a bar to an extension of such a policy to businesses generally. An act of Congress that barred individuals from interstate commerce would almost certainly be held to violate the due process clause of the Fifth Amendment. However, they could be required to procure a license subject to the same system of control as corporations so far as these were not devised especially for the latter. Corporations obtaining a license could have their internal affairs regulated by Congress, their financing controlled, and their methods of operation limited. There have not yet been enough decisions to determine what, if any, limits exist on Congress' power to impose conditions on the grant of a license to engage in interstate commerce. The opinions in the decided cases use general language only. That permits it to impose any condition which it deems appropriate for the protection of what it conceives to be the national welfare. It could be used to establish an intensive federal control over the direction of investment. This would be a most important power if national economic planning were the objective, since most businesses either produce for the interstate market or market goods that have moved in interstate commerce. It is undetermined how far it could control investment in purely local enterprises in order to protect the policy adopted by it for interstate commerce. That it could do so to some extent appears likely. The connection between a local activity and interstate commerce required to bring the former within the ambit of federal control is more easily established today than in the past.[13]

The proposed aims of economic planning include that of establishing a more just and desirable social order as well as a more stable economy. The need for the federal government to assume the lead in this movement is generally recognized. It has been doing so either alone or in cooperation with the states. Many of the regulatory measures enacted by it were in part motivated by its desire to redistribute wealth and income. Legislation strengthening the position of labor in its relations with employers reflected this attitude. Legislative price and wage fixing, whether by Congress or the states, was a more direct attempt to achieve that end. The federal power to tax is important in this connection primarily as one source of the revenues needed to finance programs to provide for the national general welfare. The other source is the power to borrow. The revenues thus obtained may be expended to finance any activity that will promote that welfare. The *Social Security Tax Cases*[14] give almost conclusive effect to the judgment of Congress as to what will achieve that objective. The use of this power has thus far been closely related to problems that arose out of the depression. This does not apply to the social security program which is intended to be permanent. Extensive programs for subsidizing both producers and consumers would be valid. The power could be used to finance public

13. The regulatory powers of Congress are as extensive with respect to foreign commerce as in the case of interstate commerce. Hence a regulation valid for the latter would be equally valid for the former.

14. C. C. Steward Machine Co. v. Davis, (1937) 301 U.S. 548; Helvering v. Davis, (1937) 301 U.S. 619.

ownership of utilities and other business enterprises in competition with privately owned enterprises. The Tennessee Valley and other similar developments can be based on it, although other federal powers have been invoked to sustain them. So far as any of such projects are not truly self-supporting they involve the same kind of redistribution of income as any other subsidy. Enough has been said to indicate the extent of the federal government's power to affect the distribution of the national income by a judicious combination of taxation, borrowing and spending.

The federal borrowing power is also one of its monetary powers. The other is that of coining money and regulating its value. It is a matter of general knowledge that a considerable part of the cost of financing the war involved monetizing a part of the debt incurred for that purpose. It is equally well known that the government's desire to keep down the cost of carrying that debt has depressed interest rates and keeps them depressed today. But for this policy general interest rates would undoubtedly be higher today than they are. Furthermore, the federal government is the only one in our system that can give its promises to pay the character of a circulating medium by giving them legal tender qualities. Congress has also plenary power over the monetary standard. This power, together with that of invalidating any and every contract deemed to interfere with a federal policy of securing a uniform currency, combine to give the federal government practically unlimited power to experiment in attempting to secure a stable economy by monetary means. But monetary manipulation or management will often, particularly to the extent that they succeed, produce a redistribution of wealth and income. That was the professed aim of the original New Deal gold policy, and the invalidation of the gold clauses effected a considerable reallocation of claims to future income as between creditors and debtors. However, the issuance of fiat money and resort to monetary management involve recognized dangers. Governments are not likely to use them to the limit unless they are exceedingly hard pressed. Hence it is probable that the federal government will concentrate on its power to spend funds raised by taxation and borrowing in furthering its social services and other methods to provide for the national general welfare. It may be noted that it does not avoid the dangers of the other methods if its borrowings become too large.

The period that witnessed this expansion of federal spending powers was also one in which the doctrine that taxes may be levied for public purposes only was greatly revised. This did not come about as the result of any reinterpretation of any provision of the federal Constitution. It was wholly a liberalizing of the "public purpose" concept found in state constitutional provisions limiting the taxing powers of the several states. This development lies outside the scope of our subject. It is noted solely because it shows that the movement for using government more and more to modify the distribution of income effected by the private enterprise economic system is due to factors of general and nationwide operation.

The increasing complexity of our social and economic system has made it practically impossible for the legislature to prescribe the precise rule that it wishes to apply to the varying facts and circumstances of all the cases which it wishes to include in its regulatory policy. It has recognized this situation and met the problem by contenting itself with formulating the policy in broad terms and conferring upon an administrative official or board the power to implement that policy for specific cases or classes of cases. Such legislation inevitably confers upon such administrators considerable discretion. The more complex the problem the greater the amount of such discretion that must be delegated if the legislative policy is to be effectively administered. It was natural that those affected by the action of administrative officials should invoke the prohibition against the delegation of legislative power. The Supreme Court had been exceedingly loath to find violations of this principle prior to 1933. Within a few years thereafter it held two important New Deal measures invalid for its violation. Since these decisions in the *Panama Refining Company*[15] and *Schechter Poultry Corporation*[16] *Cases* no federal legislation has been held invalid for that reason. The Court has invariably found the standards established by Congress for guiding administrative discretion sufficiently definite to satisfy the prohibition against delegating legislative power. In no case has it found the prescribed standard so vague as to prevent those affected thereby from knowing what lay within the administrator's power, or to interfere with adequate judicial review.[17] Some of

15. Panama Refining Co. v. Ryan, (1935) 293 U. S. 388.
16. A. L. A. Schechter Poultry Corp. v. United States, (1935) 295 U.S. 495.
17. See, for example, the following cases: Opp Cotton Mills, Inc. v. Adm'r of Wages & Hours, etc., (1941) 312 U.S. 126; United States v. Rock Royal Co-op, Inc., (1939) 307 U.S. 533; Bowles v. Willingham, (1944) 321 U.S. 503;

these decisions produced a vigorous dissent from Justice Roberts.[18] His analysis of the provisions relied upon to establish an adequate standard not only casts considerable doubt upon the majority's views but also reveals the inherent difficulties of reconciling the need to protect the individual against the petty tyrannies of a bureaucracy with that of effective government control in our modern complex social and economic organization. The net result of the recent decisions is the practical abandonment of a principle once deemed essential to achieving responsible government. It is difficult to see how any government can successfully administer the regulation of so complex an order as that which now prevails without sacrificing some of the interests which the principle against the delegation of legislative power sought to protect. It is wiser to recognize the price paid for the expansion of governmental control and planning than to deny it.

The expansion of administrative control is a normal accompaniment of the increasing governmental regulation of the national economy. It is an accepted principle of our constitutional law that those affected by administrative action have under some circumstances the right to notice and to an opportunity to be heard before any administrative determination becomes finally binding upon them. It is equally well established that they are entitled to a judicial review with respect to certain matters before being finally bound by an administrative order. The scope of the requisite review has been

---

Yakus v. United States, (1944) 321 U.S. 414; American Pr. & Lt. Co. v. Securities and Exchange Commission, (1946) 329 U.S. 90.
18. See the second, third, and fourth cases cited in note 17.

somewhat altered where rights of property only are involved. In such case the administrative findings of fact will be accepted if supported by the evidence, whether those be jurisdictional facts or otherwise. A person is still entitled to an independent judicial determination of facts of the former class in every case involving personal liberty. Since most of the regulations of the economy principally involve property rights, this change in the law deprives them of some of the protection they once received. Furthermore, the question whether the evidence in the record supports the administrative findings of fact leaves much to the reviewing court's discretion. It is felt in some quarters that courts have been too easily convinced in favor of the findings of administrative boards charged with enforcing the National Labor Relations Act. Whether or not this feeling be justified, it is undeniable that any considerable relaxation of judicial review at this point will reduce its value as a protection, especially of individual economic interests. The great increase in regulation by administrative boards, and the high degree of specialized knowledge required by many of these boards, will tend to increase the deference paid by courts to their findings of fact. Judicial abdication of the power to make independent findings of the constitutional facts in rate cases was due in some measure to judicial hesitancy to disturb the findings of experts in a highly specialized field. There is every reason to expect this attitude to extend to other equally complex economic problems. The very factors that make for increasing regulation may well reduce the value of judicial review, and in practice make the regulatory boards and commissions the dominant force in controlling the economy. It is certain that personal rights will receive more effective protection against administrative impairment than property. In no case, however, have the courts so restricted judical review as to deprive themselves of the final decision on issues of law raised by administrative action, whether they be questions of procedure or substance. There were some rather startling procedures used during the war in connection with the enforcement of the Emergency Price Control Act. Since it is not certain that they would be sustained if resorted to during peacetime, they will not be discussed.

The implications that have been herein described were developed for the most part on the basis of the decisions of the Supreme Court and the reasoning by which it supported them. Most of the decisions relied upon were rendered after 1933. However, those rendered before that date could not be and have not been ignored. They frequently fix a point of reference for measuring the extent and direction of a trend. They were important also because they furnished the Court with the tools which it employed to develop the meaning of the Constitution in its application to modern problems. A large part of the adaptation was accomplished by merely extending the application of long accepted principles. Only in rare, though important, instances were former decisions expressly overruled. The character of the data on which these implications were based must not be overlooked in appraising their meaning. Since they were developed from what are in substance propositions of law, whether or not representing the actual law as of today, they furnish no basis for forecasting the extent to which federal or state regulation of the economy will be carried nor of the direction that such regulation will take. They do not even furnish a basis for predicting the probable extent or direction of future governmental control of the economy. That will depend on many factors of which the Constitution is but one, and probably not the most important. The implications developed from propositions of law can only be other propositions of law, in this case, of federal constitutional law. They merely assert that the principles embodied in the decisions and reasoning that has been the subject of discussion imply the constitutional validity or invalidity of certain specified legislation regulating business and labor. They can be used to predict only the probable decision of our courts, more particularly the Supreme Court of the United States, were the validity of such measures before them or it for decision. They define in part the field of possible constitutional legislation. They do so only in part because not all constitutional provisions were taken into account in developing them. However, those that were taken into consideration are those that would be the most important in determining the validity of the regulatory legislation with which the discussion has been concerned. That increases the likelihood that the field delimited corresponds to the whole field of possible constitutional regulation on the basis of the present construction of those constitutional provisions. In any event, the most that these implications could establish is limits within which a planned economy is possible under the Constitution as now construed. Subsequent decisions may either expand or contract those limits. The extent to which the nation will actually move further in the direction of a planned economy depends upon more fundamental forces. The Constitution is a factor in the limited sense already indicated. Peoples' ideas about the Constitution may be even more important factors.

It is a matter of considerable controversy how far governmental economic planning is compatible with the maintenance of our other civil and political freedoms. There is no a priori answer to this question. Experience alone can give it, however difficult it may be to wring the answer from it. The matter is complicated by the fact that much depends upon the character of the plan, the extent to which planning is carried, and the methods used to implement whatever plan may be adopted. It is rendered more difficult to answer because the measures that restrict the liberty of one may expand that of another.[19] Time alone can tell whether even in such a case the increase of the latter's liberty of action. with respect to the former may not be more than offset by a restriction on his freedom through increased government control to which the plan subjects him. Whatever the ultimate answer may be, none can deny the dangers that lurk in transferring more and more power and controls to government, whether or not its members be chosen by popular election. Our nation has taken but the first steps towards government planning for the national economy. However annoying and burdensome they may have been to certain groups, or to nearly all groups during the war, they cannot yet be fairly described as having involved any general threat to the

19. See R. L. Hale, "Force and the State. A Comparison of 'Political' and 'Economic' Compulsion," 35 Col. Law Rev. 149 (1935).

civil and political liberties other than the economic of one important economic group. The very period that witnessed judicial approval of the curtailment of the economic freedom of that group has also been marked by a vigorous judicial protection of other civil liberties and of political rights. Never have freedom of speech and press and of religion been more adequately protected, with the single exception of the employer's freedom of discussion in connection with a labor dispute to which he is a party. The exception may soon be eliminated. The more that economic freedom is curtailed, the greater the value these other freedoms acquire. The more general such curtailment becomes, the greater the public necessity for preserving the others. No group can expect that limiting the economic liberty of another group for its benefit will endure forever. Hence each group has an interest in protecting the fundamental civil and political rights of every other group. Such experience as is available suggests that their preservation intact will not be easy. But unless they are protected, even to the extent of permitting opposition to the established regime by those who wish peaceably to change it, the progressive restriction of individual economic freedom may prove to be the *Road to Serfdom*[20] for even political societies imbued with the political traditions of western civilization. The danger that modern liberalism may spawn a tyrannous totalitarianism is neither an illusion nor the delusion of "reactionary" thinking.

20. See Hayek, Road to Serfdom.

Table of Cases

Index